GARDENING WITH
DROUGHT-FRIENDLY PLANTS

GARDENING WITH
DROUGHT-FRIENDLY PLANTS

TONY HALL

Kew Publishing
Royal Botanic Gardens, Kew

Royal Botanic Gardens **Kew**

© The Board of Trustees of the Royal Botanic
Gardens, Kew 2020

Photographs © Tony Hall unless otherwise stated

The author has asserted his right to be identified
as the author of this work in accordance with the
Copyright, Designs and Patents Act 1988.

All rights reserved. No part of this publication
may be reproduced, stored in a retrieval system,
or transmitted, in any form, or by any means,
electronic, mechanical, photocopying, recording
or otherwise, without written permission of the
publisher unless in accordance with the provisions
of the Copyright Designs and Patents Act 1988.

Great care has been taken to maintain the accuracy
of the information contained in this work. However,
neither the publisher nor the author can be held
responsible for any consequences arising from use of
the information contained herein.

First published in 2020 by
Royal Botanic Gardens, Kew, Richmond, Surrey,
TW9 3AE, UK
www.kew.org

Distributed on behalf of the
Royal Botanic Gardens, Kew in North America by
the University of Chicago Press,1427 East 60th St,
Chicago, IL 60637, USA.

ISBN 978 1 84246 709 1

British Library Cataloguing in Publication Data
A catalogue record for this book is available from the
British Library

Design and page layout: Kevin Knight
Project manager: Lydia White
Production manager: Jo Pillai
Copy-editing: Matthew Seal
Proofreading: Michelle Payne, Kate Dickinson

Cover image: Alliums (© Emma Crawforth)
Back cover images: *Euphorbia myrsinites* (left),
Kniphofia triangularis (right)

Printed and bound in Italy by L.E.G.O. S.p.A.

For information or to purchase all Kew titles please
visit shop.kew.org/kewbooksonline or email
publishing@kew.org

Kew's mission is to be the global resource in plant
and fungal knowledge and the world's leading
botanic garden.

Kew receives approximately one third of its funding
from Government through the Department for
Environment, Food and Rural Affairs (Defra). All
other funding needed to support Kew's vital work
comes from members, foundations, donors and
commercial activities, including book sales.

LEFT
The impressive flower
spike of *Yucca gloriosa*

Contents

ABOVE
Fruit laden loquats like this are much
more common in our warming climate

Introduction

Being a nation of garden lovers, the British like nothing better than to discuss the weather: it is variously too cold, too wet, too windy or, of course, too hot! I have gardened for 50 years and have battled against all these elements. A lesson we all learn is that we have to work with nature – we can put things in place to help the plants in our gardens, but nature and the weather will always have the last say.

I have spent a lot of time travelling around the Mediterranean studying the wild plants of that region and marvelled at their ability to withstand long dry periods with high summer temperatures and sometimes low winter temperatures. I have also experienced the Mediterranean climate zones in other countries over the past 15 years, visiting renowned wildflower sites and gardens. Many of these have shown me just how tough plants can be, and some of the extremes that they will tolerate and cope with, particularly the 'too hot and dry' bit.

With the onset of climate change, many plants that were thought not to be hardy outside the Mediterranean and Mediterranean region climate zones now grow happily elsewhere, and it is this that has inspired me to put together a list of drought-friendly plants for gardens. Whether you have a large or small garden, a courtyard, patio or balcony, there are hundreds of suitable plants.

RIGHT
Cistus are the mainstay of Kew's Mediterranean Garden, here flowering beneath a grove of olives

During my time at Kew over the last 20 years, I have seen many plants that used to grow inside the conservatories and glasshouses, which were not thought to be hardy enough to survive outside, now growing outdoors – and not just growing, in many cases thriving. Mostly this will be due to our changing, warming climate, and reduced prolonged periods of below-freezing temperatures and frost (in the south of England at least).

I well remember an old colleague of mine, Pat Smallcombe, who had spent over 40 years gardening at Kew, recalling how when they first planted out tender plants like yuccas (in what is now the Mediterranean Garden) in the late 1960s, they would wrap them with fleece every winter to protect them. Winters were generally a lot colder than they are now. However, one year they didn't get around to it for some reason. Fearing they may have lost them through the winter, the following spring it was a surprise to see the plants had suffered no ill effect through a cold winter and continued to flourish. Those same plants still sit proudly at the top of the steps in the Mediterranean Garden today, flowering every year.

It's always good to learn about the tolerance of plants to cold, wet, or drought. Yuccas, for example, have species native to a vast area, including the Americas and the Caribbean. In their case as with many others, soil conditions, not air temperatures, can make the crucial difference. Many plants including those from Mediterranean climate zones can tolerate some frost but not cold, wet ground during the winter. A good example of this is *Olea europaea*, the olive. It is grown in vast groves, both for the fruits and for olive oil production in the mountain areas of Granada where winters can be very cold and often wet, but because of the free-draining soils it has no problem coping with these conditions.

In some ways British gardeners are blessed, having soils that to some degree we can control, and weather that changes with the seasons. These mixed conditions combine to allow us to grow a wide variety of plants. In the drier, hotter parts of the world the choices are more limited, and the soils are often impoverished, rocky and almost impossible to change.

Two of the most difficult spots in gardens for plants are shady places, and areas in full sun. Both aspects can have dry soils for extended periods of time throughout the growing seasons. But full sun gives the extra stress of the sun's drying heat. This is something we're potentially going to see more of owing to global climate change in the coming years. But our changing climate isn't just about warmer temperatures, it will also feature extremes in rain, both too much rain as well as too little.

Pushing the boundaries by increasing the types of plants you grow and selecting those that will survive our changing future conditions is a challenge most adventurous gardeners will enjoy, relishing the chance to try something new and different, increasing the diversity of plants, and planting new combinations. In my own garden I have a small area dedicated to Mediterranean plants that never gets any water other than what comes out of the sky, except new plantings, which are watered until they establish. It is a joy to see how this colourful palette of plants gives year-round interest with very little work, except the odd bit of weeding, and it is an area of the garden that I never have to worry about when I'm away on holiday!

Included in this book are a range of plants that will cope with the longer dry, rainless periods that look to be our future. From the smallest of annuals and perennials, through to medium-sized trees, there is something to fit most gardens, but I've particularly had the smaller gardens in mind as they seem to be more usual with many new houses, particularly in towns and cities. However, planting can be adapted to fit any size of garden.

Gravel, courtyard or patio gardens can all lessen the stress of laborious maintenance, giving more time to enjoy these spaces in the limited free time of our busy lives. Hopefully gardening should be a pleasure, not a chore.

I hope this book will encourage and inspire the reader to push the boundaries a little. You won't always get it right, but if you don't try, you'll never know if the plant you admired on a holiday, or in a friend's garden, could grow happily for you. Give it a go…

Tolerant of dry and cold conditions, you will find *Erigeron* flowering almost all year round

Global warming/climate change

There has been a lot of debate about the reasons for the recent rise in global temperatures. There are many who think that it is just a natural Earth cycle. Over billions of years Earth has had ice ages and warm periods before, so why isn't this just another of the earth's natural cycles?

Then there are other natural phenomena like El Niño, which generally occurs every few years, when the interaction between the warmer surface temperatures of the Pacific Ocean, which are usually pushed towards the western Pacific by the trade winds, also known as tropical easterlies, increases the temperature of the atmosphere, and adds moisture. But at certain times of the year when the trade winds are weaker the warmer ocean surface water moves east, without the push of the winds.

This has the effect of thrusting the colder, denser water down below the warmed surface and to the west. This colder air in the western Pacific has little moisture content and so produces no rain, causing drought, and much wetter air in the east, formed from the warmer ocean surface drawing moisture high into the air through convection, causing rain.

Erupting volcanos can also have a major effect on weather patterns. The eruptions can send large amounts of suspended dust particles into the atmosphere, and the warmed particle-filled air rises. This reflects the sun's energy away from Earth and back into space, and so can affect weather patterns. But these are for relatively short periods of days, weeks, months and occasionally years, and are also often localised event changes.

But since the mid-twentieth century records show that there has been a rise in global temperature, which is happening faster than at any other period we know about in Earth's history, and that this increase in temperature has most likely been caused by human activities. Previous climate changes have happened over a much longer period, for example, the cooling of the ice ages.

During the Industrial Revolution, the increase in industry, fuelled by coal, oil and natural gas, saw the levels of greenhouse gases being released into the atmosphere increase dramatically.

One of the main gases was, and is, carbon dioxide. In fact, according to research, in the last 50 years the volume of this gas released into the atmosphere has increased by some 80 per cent. This has the effect of allowing the sun's light to reach the Earth's surface, but the heat is then trapped in our atmosphere, acting like the glass in a greenhouse, which is why it has been termed the 'greenhouse effect'. This trapped heat is the cause of global warming and climate change.

Some steps are being taken to help reduce some of the gas emissions, like improving energy and fuel efficiency in industry and motor vehicles, using alternative energy sources, such as water, wind and solar power, and using biofuels, instead of burning fossil fuel.

There is a worry that these changes to our climate may be happening too fast for some living things to adapt to the changes.

The trees in forests around the world absorb carbon dioxide, but many of these forests are being lost, so they are increasingly fighting a losing battle. Protecting the forests we already have and planting new ones must be a step in the right direction.

Keen gardeners have always pushed the boundaries as to what they can grow and can get away with climate-wise, but the rate at which temperatures are now rising makes it all the more important for many of us to get to know the plants that will thrive in the hotter, drier conditions that seem likely to be our future.

Dry habitats like this may be a
more common sight in the future

Plant adaptations

Plants from Mediterranean-type climates and arid and desert areas have adapted to grow in hot and dry climates. Their adaptations obviously make them very useful in a water-saving garden. Many will only need to be watered until they have established, and then little or no water will be needed. Winter rain and occasional showers throughout the year will suffice if the right plants are chosen.

Freedom from the need to continually irrigate your plants during the summer is not only good for water conservation, it also relieves the worry of being away on holidays for any length of time.

Much of the woody vegetation in Mediterranean climate regions is sclerophyllous, a term deriving from the Greek word for 'hard-leaved'. Sclerophyll vegetation generally has small, dark leaves covered with a waxy outer layer, and usually there are short distances between the leaves along the stems. Sometimes the leaves have in-rolled margins, reducing the leaf surface. These adaptations all help to retain moisture in the dry summer months.

Some plants are summer deciduous, meaning they lose their leaves in the summer. Examples are *Euphorbia dendroides* and *Calicotome villosa* (in the pea family), which when among most green plants during summer look like they have succumbed to the summer heat. This strategy reduces the energy and water demand of the plant and helps to conserve water during summer drought.

Many countries with Mediterranean climates have impoverished soils that are often not much more than

Looking dead but very much alive, *Euphorbia* shows summer dormancy, shedding all of its leaves to conserve valuable water

rocks and stones, as well as brutal, scorching heat throughout the summer months, with cloudless skies giving the sun's full attention to plants that grow beneath it. This all sounds like a recipe for disaster, but many plants have evolved and adapted to grow and grow well in these conditions.

On the other hand, the UK has generally nutrient-rich soils with good amounts of rainfall throughout the year, including some during most summers. In much of the Mediterranean this is almost unheard of!

You might expect that in these more favourable conditions there would be a good number of British native plant species compared with the more hostile plant-growing conditions of some Mediterranean climate zones.

In actual fact in the Mediterranean Basin there are around 25,000 species of plants growing, many of them tolerating summer drought. It is one of the richest areas of plant diversity in the world.

I have botanised in California and South West Australia, and have South Africa on my 'still to travel to' list, although familiar with the flora. I have travelled around much of the Mediterranean Basin, with my main focus in the provinces of Andalucía, in southern Spain,

where the plant diversity in the drier areas is absolutely amazing, and where in some regions they have many rainless months where temperatures are often reaching over 40 °C (104 °F). Parts of the province of Almeria in the south-east corner of Spain are desert-like, and have the lowest rainfall of anywhere in Europe, with 200 mm (8 in) as an annual average. This compares to Britain's average of 1,154 mm (45 in) a year.

A typical region around the Mediterranean Basin has hot, dry summers and cool, moist or wet winters, with rare or short-lived frosts and snow only on the higher mountain areas. There are four other areas with Mediterranean climate-like zones around the world determined by their latitude. This is approximately 30–40 degrees latitude both north and south of the equator and includes western and southern Australia, California, Chile and South Africa.

The five Mediterranean-climate regions of the world occupy less than five per cent of the Earth's surface, yet they harbour more than 48,000 known vascular plant species, which is almost 20 per cent of the world total.

Many of the plants profiled in this book originate in these Mediterranean regions. Each region has its own type of vegetation, which I will describe briefly.

Mediterranean flora: Maquis & garigue

Maquis is a dense scrub vegetation, which can become almost impenetrable. It is made up of mainly evergreen small trees and shrubs to around 3 m (10 ft) in height. In low pH areas this can be dominated by *Arbutus* and heathers, while in higher pH areas plants like *Phillyrea* species and *Quercus coccifera* dominate.

Garigue is generally a much more open vegetation, made up of many low-growing woody shrubs, from around 30 cm (12 in) to 1 m (3 ft) high, with clearings in between. It is characterised by many aromatic plants, like rosemary, thymes and lavenders. Because it is a more open vegetation, a wide variety of herbaceous plants like orchids, annuals and bulbous plants add colour in the clearings, particularly in the spring.

This is a type of habitat and flora that lends itself well to gravel gardens.

Australian flora: Mallee

Mallee vegetation comes from a biogeographic region in western Australia that has a semi-arid Mediterranean-type climate, where plants grow in sandy soils with very little and unreliable rainfall. The main plants are low-growing multi-stemmed eucalyptus species like *Eucalyptus dumosa*, which after fires are able to re-sprout from underground lignotubers, which store carbohydrates and water. Other plants that dominate in this vegetation are acacias, *Hakea* and *Melaleuca* species, along with hummock grasses and the endemic *Kingia australis*. Many rare and endemic plants grow throughout this habitat.

ABOVE
Natural garigue. Nature's dry garden,
a mix of shrubs, bulbs and grasses

Californian flora: Chaparral

Chaparral is a plant community growing in heath and shrubland, which is semi-arid. As in most other Mediterranean areas, the plants are mainly woody with leaves adapted to summer drought (sclerophyllous). These leaves are thick and waxy, which helps reduce dehydration. The shrubland vegetation is mainly made up of evergreen shrubs and small trees to around 2.5 m (8 ft) tall, like the Californian scrub oak, *Quercus berberidifolia*, and the sagebush, *Artemisia californica*, which with other plants form dense thickets.

Chilean flora: Matorral

Chilean matorral vegetation is found on the west coast of South America, in a narrow 1,000 km (620 mile) band in north-central Chile. It lies between the Pacific Ocean to the west and the southern Andes to the east. The Atacama Desert, which is one of the driest areas in the world, lies to the north. Here the main vegetation types are deciduous thorn scrub with columnar cacti, *Echinopsis* and *Eulychnia* species. There is more evergreen woodland as you travel south, which includes palms such as the endemic tall *Jubaea chilensis*. Like many other Mediterranean-like climates, it has a single rainy season, with as much as six months of drought.

South African flora: Fynbos

The vegetation in South Africa's south-western Cape mountains is mostly fynbos, one of the world's most

ABOVE
Kingia australis. Endemic to western Australia with their striking and distinctive grass-like topped trunks

remarkable vegetation types. This is an area with plants that are adapted to hot, dry summers and frequent fires.

The fynbos has no real dormant season (unlike Namaqualand's stunning, but brief, spring displays) and is dominated by evergreen plants with needle-like leaves, such as those in the Ericaceae family, which with their reduced leaf surface are designed to withstand drought through evapotranspiration, and the Proteaceae. Many plants in the Proteaceae family have flat leaves that have no distinct upper or lower leaf surfaces, and they often face upwards, shading themselves from the midday sun in the hottest parts of the year, exposing only their narrow leaf margins. There is also a very high percentage of endemic plants and families, like Penaeaceae. This family includes *Brachysiphon microphyllus*, which grows in sandstone cracks and fissures, with roots that reach deep down into these cracks to moist areas below. Many fynbos bulbs also bury themselves deeply in these fissures in the accumulation of moist humus that builds up.

Samantha Muir / Alamy Stock Photo

Plant adaptations to cope with harsh conditions

Some plants in hot and dry areas reduce both leaf size and leaf surface area, by rolling the sides under. This can be seen in plants like rosemary. Grasses like *Stipa*, with their long, narrow leaves, also have this reduced leaf surface. By having a smaller leaf surface, they lessen the amount of water lost through the leaves in a process called evapotranspiration (including both evaporation and transpiration). Xerophytes like cacti have very few leaves. Their leaves have been reduced and adapted into thorns or spines, and the pads we think of as their leaves are actually thickened stems, which store water to use when needed during prolonged dry periods.

Stomata are holes in a leaf through which water evaporates. Some plants will open their stomata at night and close them before the heat of the day, so reducing evaporation. This is the opposite of what happens in plants that do not have to deal with drought conditions.

Some plants are summer deciduous. An example is the Mediterranean legume, *Calicotome spinosa*. This plant produces leaves and flowers from early spring to early summer. But during the hotter summer months it drops all its leaves, completely reducing any water loss, coming back into leaf during cooler and wetter periods.

Some geraniums, like *Geranium malviflorum*, are summer dormant. This type of plant can be useful in the garden for giving an early display and then making room for other later summer- flowering plants.

The majority of bulbs, corms, rhizomes and tubers known as geophytes are somewhat like the summer deciduous shrubs in losing their leaves in summer, and like herbaceous perennials in dying back to ground

OPPOSITE TOP
Creosote bush, *Larrea tridentata* in the Californian desert

OPPOSITE BELOW
An endemic cactus, *Copiapoa carrizalensis* growing in the Atacama Desert, Chile

ABOVE
Fynbos vegetation on the Cape Peninsula

level. They grow and flower in spring and early summer, becoming dormant as underground storage organs before the scorching and drying summer heat, regrowing in more favourable conditions. This lifestyle makes them a useful plant in drought-resistant gardens. Some also flower during autumn, during cooling temperatures and the first rains.

Annuals also have drought-beating qualities. As their name suggests, they complete their life cycle within one year. Mature plants shed their seed at the end of their growing cycle, usually in early summer. This seed survives until the rains come the following season, when the plants germinate, grow, flower and set seed, completing their annual cycle again. In particularly dry regions seed can lay dormant for many years, until reawakened by rain.

Plants from a group known as Phreatophytes grow in extreme desert conditions, surviving by growing long tap roots. The roots of this type of plant extend deep down into the soil and sand to find the water table, so always have a supply of water. Some plants, like the velvet mesquite tree (*Prosopis velutina*), a legume from the desert regions of northern Mexico and the south-western United States of America, can reach down as far as 25 m (82 ft) to find available water. Examples of more common native UK plants that have this characteristic and do very well in drought conditions are sea kale (*Crambe maritima*) and sea holly (*Eryngium* spp.).

A common leaf colour of many small shrubs and perennials in the Mediterranean is grey and silver. Leaves that appear to be grey and silver are actually normal green leaves, but covered in fine, tiny hairs.

ABOVE LEFT
Opuntia. The swollen pads or stems of cacti are adapted to store water to see them through long dry periods

ABOVE CENTRE
Dormant bulbs. The huge, dormant sun-baked bulbs of *Drimia maritima*, waiting for cooler weather to resume growth

These hairs have two functions: they trap moisture, and they also reflect some of the high light levels and heat away from the leaves. *Stachys* is commonly known as lamb's ears owing to it being covered in a coat of dense hairs that make it soft to the touch. This dense covering of hairs also helps reduce evaporation.

Succulent plants like sedums and aloes have adapted their stems and/or leaves into water-storing vessels, with a surface that is often covered in a waxy resin. This gives them a glaucous appearance, which may also help reflect sunlight.

A memory is stuck in my mind. I made a spring trip to Cadiz province in Andalucía in 2001. On one of my walks I came across a small area, around about one-third the size of a football pitch, with a rocky outcrop, and remember being wowed by the amount of plant diversity and colour in such a small area. There were blues, yellows, whites, reds and pinks. There were so many plants, many of which I didn't know at the time. I remember thinking if I could just lift this natural garden that nature had created, and take it home, it would be the most amazing Mediterranean garden (not that I had a third of a football pitch at my disposal). This was an area that was obviously never watered, apart from what fell naturally from the skies. Sadly, developers didn't see it in the same way I did, and it has now gone, to be replaced with concrete…

With this area in mind I redeveloped the Mediterranean Garden at Kew, as well as my own small dry garden at home.

Many gardens look similar when it comes to plant choice, because people tend to stick to a safe palette of plants, and this is partly dictated by the garden centre chains. But there is already a trend in the plants available towards more Mediterranean-type and drought-resistant plants. Using plants that will suit our changing climate has to be the way forward. There is an incredible range from which you can create an attractive labour- and water-saving garden that will also be attractive to bees and butterflies.

ABOVE
Stachys byzantina 'Silver Carpet'. Minute hairs cover the surface of the leaves, reflecting sunlight and reducing transpiration

Low-maintenance gardens

It seems that the pace of life becomes increasingly hectic and fast, so our limited free time is to be treasured. A garden space, whatever its size, should be a place for relaxation and contemplation. Gardening is an enjoyable activity, but it also can also be quite time-consuming. So if you have limited time then a low-maintenance garden, or more appropriately, an easy maintenance garden (because all gardens need some maintenance), is worth considering.

Paving a garden over is many people's answer to low maintenance, but our changing climate looks likely to produce increased periods of heavy rainfall, and too much paving may lead to flooding, making the garden unusable for periods of time. It's better to have a mix of paved and un-paved areas, this will allow rainwater to naturally soak away.

One of the most time-consuming areas of any garden to look after is the lawn, and the finer the lawn the more time and amount of work is needed to keep it looking good. Reducing the size of lawn area might help, but smaller lawns don't necessarily mean less work. They are generally fiddlier, so in actual fact can be more work – and time-consuming.

Lawns also need a lot of water to keep them green during the summer, and this is something responsible gardeners should try to avoid. Grasses that are made up of an 'Amenity' seed mix are harder wearing, and even though they will go completely brown in a dry summer, they will recover during autumn.

Perhaps a better alternative, if you want grass, is an area of long grass that once established takes very little management and maintenance. This is also good for wildlife, especially if planted with a mix of wildflowers, and generally only needs cutting once a year, after the flowers have faded and have set and dispersed their seed. Long grass generally holds on to moisture longer, so lasts better in dry summers, but also looks good, even when dry.

Mulch is a great help in a water-saving garden and a low-maintenance gardener's best friend. There are many types to choose from, both organic and inorganic.

Using containers in a garden is a great way of growing plants that may not be fully hardy, as they can be brought out during the summer and then put back into a conservatory or greenhouse for the winter months. It is also a good way of moving seasonal colour around to areas of the garden that may have a temporary need for a bit of a lift. And of course, they will be the mainstay of many patio and courtyard gardens. Pots and containers do take a little more time and effort when it comes to watering. But by using large containers, which hold a greater volume of compost, and using a soil-based compost that will stay wet longer, you can lessen the frequency of the need to water.

Choosing a selection of hardy plants as the main plants in a garden is the best option, as they will obviously

need less attention, but I would always have space for a few 'potentially' hardy plants, because gardening is all about continual learning, and making a few mistakes along the way is all part of this learning. And hopefully some plants will turn out to be hardier than you thought.

Having plants that can more or less look after themselves, once established, is an obvious advantage in any garden. It's worth pushing the boundaries and trying new plants, and sometimes you will just need to find the right niche for a particular plant in your garden. Not everything will work and there will always be a bit of trial and error, but using the plants and methodology suggested in this book will help you lessen maintenance time and create a garden for all seasons.

Dry and gravel gardens are low maintenance, and with good plant choices look good all year round

Small gardens

Gardens are getting proportionally smaller, particularly in new housing developments. In any case, town and city gardens have always been generally smaller than gardens in suburbia. The lack of space afforded by a small garden shouldn't be seen as a problem but as a challenge to be a bit more thoughtful and creative in your choice of landscaping and plants, and an advantage of a small garden is less maintenance, if good plant choices are made.

Courtyard gardens

Courtyard gardens tend to be the smallest of garden spaces, so aspect is very important, especially for plant placement. During the summer months when the sun is high in the sky, much of the courtyard could be in sun for much of the day, but during the winter months the lower sun might not reach some parts of the garden at all.

Gardeners should try to use as much of the space as possible, without cluttering. Walls can be used for climbers – *Trachelospermum jasminoides*, the star jasmine, is evergreen with wonderfully scented flowers – or maybe even a living wall. Many systems are available in kit form. A living wall can still be drought resistant if using plants like *Sempervivum* with water-wise systems.

Containers are an option, and you can grow annual climbers in pots, for example *Ipomoea purpurea* (morning glory), giving colour, height and a tropical feel. Shrubs like *Fatsia* do particularly well in containers in the shadier parts of a garden. Small trees such as olives, bays and palms have good drought resistance. These can be set up with a watering system to look after your plants while you are away. Having a water butt in the courtyard saves water and is easily accessible in the area where you need it.

Bamboos also make great container plants, adding a different form and texture, but will need a little more water if positioned in full sun.

Courtyards can also be frost-free, and create a microclimate that allows more tender plants, such as bananas, to grow outside year round, creating a quiet oasis.

Patio gardens

Growing plants in containers is not only a way of planting up areas of hard landscape, but also a way of extending the type of plants that can be grown. Many plants from the Mediterranean areas are hardy above ground; what often kills them when planted in the ground over winter is cold, wet soils, which their roots will not tolerate. Containerising them gives you the option of planting in good, open, free-draining composts, adjusted for either acid- or alkaline-loving plants. This would be difficult in a planted bed with just one soil type, and you have the ability to move the more tender plants away for more protection.

Courtyard garden. Pretty courtyard garden, growing tender plants protected from frost

There are many advantages in growing plants in pots and containers, the pots and containers themselves often being as much as a feature as the plants. They can help soften hard areas, add height and colour, and you can move them around to try out different combinations and ideas, which is not so easy with plants planted in more permanent beds. Seasonal interest can be extended by just adding annuals or bulbs to existing containers, giving an extra splash of colour and a greater degree of flexibility.

Watering is of course an issue for plants grown in containers, but they are remarkably easy to look after once you have established their requirements. Often there are indicator plants that will be the first to show signs of dryness during summer months, prompting you to water slightly more during these periods. Pots and containers can also be mulched with organic or inorganic materials, such as bark chips or gravel, which will help conserve water loss through surface evaporation.

Plants have been grown in pots for millennia – the ancient Greeks and Romans were known to have grown citrus trees in pots on paved areas. Archaeological digs have recovered pots that look remarkably similar to those used today.

Vary the size of your pots, mixing large with small, but use materials that complement each other and their surroundings, so as not to look too random. Using too many small pots gives a cluttered feel to a space. Just because your area may be small doesn't mean the plants, pots and containers have to be! Make sure they are frost resistant.

Bigger pots and containers are better. Apart from their impact, they more importantly are a more water-wise approach. They hold more water for longer, having more

soil, and it's easier to fit modern watering systems, like water reservoirs, to them.

With some good forward planning, whether you have a windowsill, a balcony, roof garden, small city garden, a gravelled front drive, patio or courtyard garden, there are plants and containers to suit.

Gravel gardens

The gravel garden is my favourite type of garden, most probably because of my fondness for the Mediterranean.

ABOVE
Euphorbia milii. Succulents do well in containers and generally need less watering

I love the way the ground cover colours of gravel make each plant somehow showier, much more so than when the same plant is planted in a conventional border, and particularly when grown through the textured, honey-tones of limestone gravel.

Selection of the gravel is important. Pea gravel may be the most attractive to some, especially for small areas, but cats tend to also find this attractive too, as a huge litter tray! Choosing a larger-sized chipping will deter this, and is also easier to walk on. Best of all is a mixture of sizes, as these will bind together better and travel less.

As well as size, try to match the colour of any paving to the colour of the gravel, and vice versa. Ideally the gravel chippings should be put on to a depth of between 5 and 7.5 cm (2 to 3 in). This should be borne in mind when planting as some smaller plants will need to be planted high to compensate for when the gravel is added.

For me a gravel garden should be planted fairly sparsely to keep the planting as natural looking as possible. Try not to plant in too organised a fashion, keeping it loose and open, with plenty of gravel visible, allowing things to self-seed. Always keep an eye out for aggressive weeds, removing them while they are small. When establishing a new gravel garden, you need to ensure that you have removed all perennial weeds, as these are more difficult to deal with than the annual weeds that will inevitably seed themselves among the gravel, and are easily removed.

You can lay down a fabric membrane prior to planting, cutting crossed slits to plant through, and then put your gravel over it. I find plants do much better without this, however, particularly if the soil isn't free-draining, as the fabric holds up the water from penetrating the soil. This can lead to some rotting off when establishing plants, and

in the worst case encourage moss to grow. It also hinders the plants you do want to self-seed naturally, and which root down between pure gravel much more easily.

Generally most Mediterranean-type plants grow in impoverished soil, so there is no need to enrich the soil unless adding organic material to improve the drainage of clay soils. If you are lucky enough to have good, free-draining, sandy soil, it will benefit the range of plants you can grow. In rich soils Mediterranean plants will grow unnaturally lush and outgrow their space quickly, meaning they will need regular pruning, spoiling their natural appearance and that of the garden generally.

ABOVE
Lavender is a great plant for gravel gardens, being drought-tolerant and attractive to bees and butterflies

Plant list

The plants described in the following list are in alphabetical order within their categories, with both their botanical and common names. Many are plants that I have seen growing in the wild, and all are plants that I have studied in both private and public gardens, with an emphasis on those I work with daily in the Royal Botanic Gardens, Kew. They are all plants that are tried and tested for their ability, once established, to cope with summer dry conditions, and many will also tolerate differing degrees of low temperatures.

The range of their flowering times covers an approximate period depending on the location in which they are growing, as well as yearly and seasonal differences in weather and temperature.

The main focus for all of the plants described is their use in water-wise and low-maintenance gardens. But they also need to have a degree of hardiness to be included here, so all have a hardiness rating indicating the coldest temperature the plants will tolerate. This rating is for the parts of the plant that are above soil level, and many of them will not tolerate cold, wet soil conditions. Good drainage is key. Smaller gardens, particularly those in built-up areas, will benefit some of the plants that are on the tender side, as they offer more shelter and a beneficial microclimate.

The height and spread of each plant is also given. These are for the plant's mature size. Plants that are unfamiliar can be difficult to place in a design, and it's important to allow the correct distance between young plants to give them the space they need to grow into without crowding each other out.

At the end of each description is the pruning requirement of each plant, if needed. Good pruning will produce strong-growing plants, lessen the chance of disease and encourage flowering.

OPPOSITE
Small yellow button-like flowers of *Santolina* stand out against their silver-grey foliage

ABOVE
False dittany grown for its yellow-green foliage

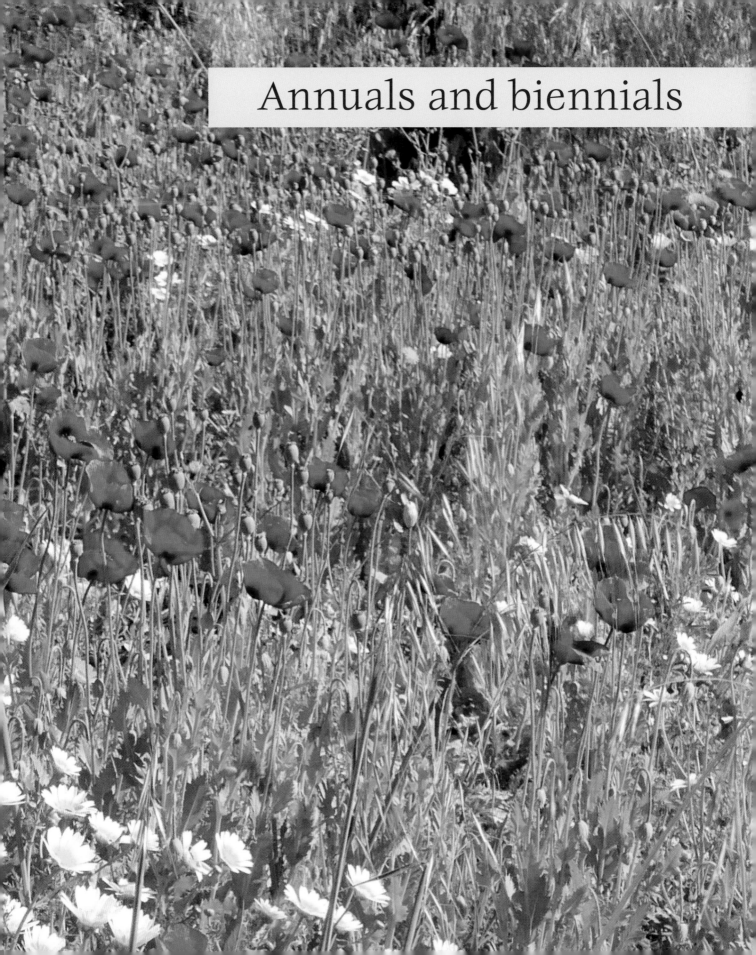

Annuals and biennials

Cerinthe major '**Purpurascens**'

CERINTHE MAJOR
Honeywort
BORAGINACEAE

Cerinthe major 'Purpurascens' is the most commonly grown honeywort. It has glaucous, blue-green, fleshy, oval leaves, often mottled with white markings. Its upright stems arch over at their tops to reveal attractive, rich, purple tubular flowers with a pale, wavy margin, hanging from within equally attractive blue bracts. These unusual-looking plants will self-seed themselves around the garden but are easily removed from unwanted areas. They are also a great plant for attracting bees into the garden.

ASPECT: Full sun to partial shade.
FLOWERING: May – July.
HARDINESS: 1 to -5 °C (34 to 23 °F).

 30–60 cm (12–24 in)

10–30 cm (4–12 in)

PREVIOUS PAGE
A colourful wildflower
display of annual poppies

Cleome '**Helen Campbell**'

CLEOME
Spider flower
CLEOMACEAE

Cleome cultivars come in a wide range of colours, but mainly whites, pinks and red. Many are from the species *Cleome hassleriana*, native to South America, which in the wild produces flowers that are mainly pink, and also purple and white. It is from these that a range of cultivars have arisen, like the pure white 'Helen Campbell'.

Cleome is treated as a half-hardy annual, although it will sometimes re-seed itself in the garden, producing new plants the following year. It is best started from seed early in the year and planted out after all risk of frost has passed. Once established they are drought-tolerant, producing large flowerheads made up of numerous individual flowers with long whisker-like stamens, on tall erect stems. Deadheading the flowers encourages a longer flowering period, but they should continue flowering until the first frosts.

ASPECT: Full sun.
FLOWERING: June – September.
HARDINESS: 1 to 5 °C (34 to 41 °F).

 1–1.5 m (3–5 ft)

10–30 cm (4–12 in)

ECHIUM
Vipers bugloss

BORAGINACEAE

Echiums produce a wide range of wonderful plants that have the wow factor, from huge towering giant tree echiums such as *Echium pininana*, with spires up to 5 m (16 ft) tall (Ventnor Botanic Garden, on the Isle of Wight, and Tresco Abbey Gardens have always had magnificent displays of this echium), to the much smaller but equally as impressive *Echium albicans* from the mountains of Andalucía.

ECHIUM ALBICANS – is an upright biennial, which produces a basal rosette of overlapping silver-grey leaves, which overwinter, and then in the following spring produces a flower spike up to 50 cm (20 in) tall. The stems, stalks and flower buds are all covered in long, white hairs, giving the

The towering blue flower spikes of *Echium pininana* are a magnet for bees and butterflies

Echium pininana

Echium albicans

whole plant a silvery effect. The flowers are pink, through to bluish-purple, changing colour with age, and opening from the bottom up.

I grow this plant in the Mediterranean Garden at Kew, and it is probably the plant I get asked about most.

ECHIUM PININANA – is a truly impressive plant, a plant with attitude! Towering above most of the shrubs, it is extremely showy. Like many of the echiums, it is a biennial plant, producing its flowering spike up to 5 m (16 ft) in the second year before setting seed and dying. Unfortunately, it is not fully hardy, but is definitely worth trying, and hopefully it will find a niche in a sheltered spot where it will grow well.

I found that by growing them in pots the first year and then planting them out they flowered and set seed. Lots

of seedlings came from these, and a few survived into the second year and flowered. So now every year I get a few that make it to flower.

ECHIUM WILDPRETII – is even less hardy than *Echium pininana*, but it is such a beautiful plant with its deep-pink flowering spike, up to 2 m (7 ft) tall, above silver-grey foliage, that I treat it as a bedding plant. I grow it in pots under cover for the first year and plant it out in its second flowering season, collecting seed and repeating the process. I think it's well worth the effort, and so do our visitors.

ASPECT: Full sun to partial shade.
FLOWERING: April – July.
HARDINESS: 1 to -5 °C (34 to 23 °F).

Indicated individually

Indicated individually

Planted in large drifts, *Nigella* has real flower-power

Nigella damascena

GLAUCIUM FLAVUM
Yellow horned poppy
PAPAVERACEAE

A very distinctive and showy member of the poppy family. The yellow horned poppy is a short-lived perennial, but more usually grown as a biennial. *Glaucium* is a plant of the seashores and is a British native wildflower, still fairly common around our coastal shingle beaches. It is also native in northern Europe and the Mediterranean. It is a plant for full sun and cannot tolerate shade.

Large branching heads of lemon-yellow cupped flowers centred with bright yellow stamens are held above the waxy blue-grey foliage, which has a deeply crumpled appearance. It is from the long, upright, horn-like seed pods that it gets its common name.

All parts of this plant are poisonous, and when cut or broken it exudes a yellow sap.

ASPECT: Full sun.
FLOWERING: June – September.
HARDINESS: -5 to -10 °C (23 to 14 °F).

 50–75 cm (20–30 in)

10–50 cm (4–20 in)

NIGELLA DAMASCENA
Love-in-a-mist
RANUNCULACEAE

An upright bushy annual, with wonderfully fine, feathery foliage. Sky-blue flowers are held on upright stems above fine bracts and have many overlapping petals in the semi-double form, with the stamens raised unusually high in the centre, adding to their attractiveness.

'Miss Jekyll' is a reliable blue cultivar. You can also get pink, purple and white varieties. Like most hardy annuals they will seed themselves around, but are easily controlled by removing seedlings, or unripe seed heads, although both the flowers and seed heads make attractive cut and dried flowers for use in arrangements.

ASPECT: Full sun.
FLOWERING: June – September.
HARDINESS: 1 to -5 °C (34 to 23 °F).

 30–50 cm (12–20 in)

10–30 cm (4–12 in)

OPPOSITE *Glaucium flavum*

Bulbs

AGAPANTHUS
African bell lilies
AMARYLLIDACEAE

Agapanthus includes a wide range of species and colours, both evergreen and deciduous perennials, but it is the deciduous ones that are the hardier and most drought-friendly. The evergreen types such as *Agapanthus* 'Peter Pan' will still get through most winters but will lose their leaves in the coldest winters, and both evergreen and deciduous types benefit from mulching to give some protection during the colder months.

As with many plants the common names can be confusing. Two of the most used common names for *Agapanthus* are African bell lilies and lily of the Nile. In fact, they are not lilies at all and are actually in the same family as daffodils (Amaryllidaceae), and native to southern Africa.

They make excellent container plants when grown in large pots, flowering best when a little restricted, but should be divided or potted up to larger containers every three years or so.

There are hundreds of varieties and cultivars including ones with bicolour flowers, like *Agapanthus* 'Twister', which has a blue base to each flower, turning white at the petal tips, and some with variegated leaves, as well as dwarf varieties growing to around 40 cm (16 in) and tall varieties to almost 1 m (3 ft) tall.

AGAPANTHUS AFRICANUS – Deep blue (evergreen)

AGAPANTHUS AFRICANUS 'ALBUS' – White, tinged pink (evergreen)

AGAPANTHUS AFRICANUS 'TWISTER' – Blue and white (evergreen)

Heads of trumpet-shaped flowers in a variety of colours make *Agapanthus* a great addition to any border

Agapanthus

AGAPANTHUS CAMPANULATUS 'ALBOVITTATUS' – Variegated, pale blue flowers (evergreen)

AGAPANTHUS CAMPANULATUS 'COBALT BLUE' – Violet-blue (deciduous)

AGAPANTHUS CAMPANULATUS 'ROSEWARNE' – Sky blue flowers (evergreen)

AGAPANTHUS HEADBOURNE HYBRIDS – Raised in the 1940s in Hampshire, they are variable in colour, from light to dark blue (deciduous)

AGAPANTHUS INAPERTUS 'GRASKOP' – Dark violet-blue (deciduous)

AGAPANTHUS INAPERTUS 'MIDNIGHT CASCADE' – Black buds open to deep purple flowers (deciduous)

AGAPANTHUS INAPERTUS 'SKY' – Pendulous, sky blue (deciduous)

AGAPANTHUS UMBELLATUS 'BLUE GIANT' – As the name suggests, large heads of blue flowers (evergreen)

AGAPANTHUS 'ARCTIC STAR' – White flowers (deciduous)

AGAPANTHUS 'GOLDEN DROP' – Low-growing, compact variety, pale blue flowers with golden-edged foliage (evergreen)

AGAPANTHUS 'LOCH HOPE' – Narrow leaves beneath deep blue flowers (deciduous)

AGAPANTHUS 'NORTHERN STAR' – Dark, violet-blue flowers, with striped petals (deciduous)

AGAPANTHUS 'WINDSOR GREY' – Unusual, greyish-white to pale lavender flowers (deciduous).

ASPECT: Full sun.

FLOWERING: July – September.

HARDINESS: -5 to -10 °C (23 to 14 °F).

 30 cm–1.5 m (1–5 ft)

50 cm (20 in)

PREVIOUS PAGE
The huge flower filled heads of alliums

OPPOSITE *Agapanthus campanulatus* 'Cobalt Blue'

Cutting back the spent flowering stem is all the care that is needed.

ASPECT: Full sun.

FLOWERING: June – August.

HARDINESS: -5 to -10 °C (23 to 14 °F).

 10 cm–1 m (4 in–3 ft)

10–50 cm (4–20 in)

MUSCARI NEGLECTUM
Common grape hyacinth

ASPARAGACEAE

This small, bulbous perennial plant flowers early in the year and is extremely hardy. I have seen it growing in the Spanish mountains where snow and freezing conditions are commonplace, and then at the opposite extreme being baked in hot, dry, stony soils in the summer.

The pretty little flowers are borne on erect, slender stems, above spreading, lax leaves. The flowers are in a terminal cluster, resembling tiny bunches of grapes. The lower flowers are deep blue, almost blackish, becoming much paler at the top of the cluster. It is not the earliest bulb to flower in the year, but always a welcome sight as spring progresses.

ASPECT: Full sun and partial shade.

FLOWERING: March – May.

HARDINESS: -10 to -15 °C (14 to 5 °F).

 10–20 cm (4–8 in)

5–10 cm (2–4 in)

NARCISSUS PAPYRACEUS
Paper-white daffodil

AMARYLLIDACEAE

My own little patch of dry garden sits right outside my kitchen window, and for me it is a real joy in the depths of winter to see this little daffodil looking back at me. In the Mediterranean it is brought into the houses as a cut flower at Christmas where its sweet fragrance can

Narcissus papyraceus

be enjoyed. In the UK it is also often in flower in December.

The pure white flowers are produced in clusters of up to ten individual overlapping blooms, with bright yellow stamens in the small, central, cup-like corolla.

ASPECT: Full sun and partial shade.

FLOWERING: December – April.

HARDINESS: -5 to -10 °C (23 to 14 °F).

 20–40 cm (8–16 in)

5–10 cm (2–4 in)

ORNITHOGALUM NARBONENSE
Star of Bethlehem

ASPARAGACEAE

Star of Bethlehem is a common sight in much of the Mediterranean, particularly on land that has been abandoned and in the cleared areas of old olive groves.

Flowering in the spring, it produces a single, pyramidal, branched, flowering spike that opens from the bottom up, and has up to 30 individual star-like, six-petalled white flowers, which have a broad green central stripe on each petal. The stripe is much more prominent on

Ornithogalum narbonense

the undersides, making the unopened flower buds very attractive. Best planted in small groups and will multiply quite quickly.

ASPECT: Full sun.

FLOWERING: May – July.

HARDINESS: -5 to -10 °C (23 to 14 °F).

 30–50 cm (12–20 in)

5–10 cm (2–4 in)

SCILLA PERUVIANA
Portuguese squill
ASPARAGACEAE

A late spring-flowering bulbous perennial with semi-evergreen broad, dark green, lance-shaped leaves. Its epithet *peruviana* might suggest it is a native of Peru, but in fact it is a plant native to the western Mediterranean. It is thought that when the bulbs first arrived in the UK, they were on a ship called *Peru*, which was presumed to have sailed from South America but had in fact come from the Mediterranean, and this is where the confusion arose.

It is such a pretty plant when in flower, each bulb producing a large, single flowerhead that contains up to 100 individual small, violet-blue, six-petalled, star-like flowers, opening from the outside edge first and towards the centre. The darker unopened central buds contrast well with the already opened outer flowers. As the flowers mature, they become taller, revealing the separate short flowering stems of individual flowers.

A general rule of thumb with most bulbs is that they are planted at twice their depth. With *Scilla peruviana* they are better planted with their tips just below the surface. In their native habitats you will often find them growing with some of their bulb exposed above ground, but this is in areas where there is no risk of frost. Over time they should naturalise and produce small clumps.

Scilla peruviana also makes a good plant for growing in containers.

ASPECT: Full sun.

FLOWERING: April – June.

HARDINESS: -10 to -15 °C (14 to 5 °F).

10–30 cm (4–12 in)

10–30 cm (4–12 in)

Large flowerheads of up to 100 individual violet-blue, star-like flowers

Scilla peruviana

TULBAGHIA VIOLACEA
Society garlic
AMARYLLIDACEAE

A pretty little plant, which will slowly spread, forming small clumps by means of underground rhizomes. This is a recent addition to my garden and a plant that I have already become very fond of.

The slender grey-green leaves smell of garlic when bruised, and from within these the pale purple, or lilac-coloured fragrant flowers are held in clusters on tall bare stems, of a dozen or so individual little blooms, resembling miniature *Agapanthus* flowers. They have a really long flowering season, from early summer right through into the autumn. Both the leaves and the flowers are edible.

ASPECT: Full sun.

FLOWERING: June – November.

HARDINESS: 0 to -5 °C (32 to 23 °F).

20–50 cm (8–20 in)

10–50 cm (4–20 in)

Tulbaghia violacea

OPPOSITE
Bursting with summer promise, an allium flowerhead

AKEBIA QUINATA
Chocolate vine
LARDIZABALACEAE

A lovely semi-evergreen climber that despite its tender look is surprisingly tolerant of both high and low temperatures. The twining stems need some support to train them against a wall, fence or over a pergola, where it can easily reach 4 m (13 ft) in height or length.

The three- or five-lobed leaves appear bright green and contrast well with the unusual-looking fragrant flowers, which smell like spicy chocolate. These appear in spring and have three plum-purple-coloured cupped petals that almost reflex with age. Each is centred with six darker purple-brown stamens. These female flowers are much larger and showier than the male flowers, which grow on the same plant. To produce the long, sausage-shaped fruits you will need a second plant for cross-pollination.

I have an established example of this plant that I inherited and have not watered for more than ten years. So apart from rain it is on its own, and it flourishes and flowers every year.

Akebia can be quite vigorous, but trimming to keep them in their allotted space rather than any heavy pruning is generally all that is required. This should be done in late spring after flowering.
ASPECT: Full sun to partial shade.
FLOWERING: April – June.
HARDINESS: -15 to -20 °C (5 to -4 °F).

8–12 m (26–39 ft)

8–12 m (26–39 ft)

CAMPSIS RADICANS
Trumpet vine
BIGNONIACEAE

A large deciduous climber that is self-clinging to walls by aerial roots that are produced along its stems. But it does need

Akebia quinata

Campsis radicans f. *flava*

some initial support until established. It can also be trained over an arbour or pergola. Leaves are dark, glossy green and made up of 9 or 11 toothed leaflets. The large orange and red trumpet-shaped flowers are produced all summer and borne in terminal clusters of usually between five and ten flowers, which individually can be up to 8 cm (3 in) long, and are loved by bees and other insects.

There is also a yellow form, *Campsis radicans* f. *flava*, which has equally large flowers, also borne in terminal clusters during the summer.

It is a climber that definitely needs growing space and will easily spread 3 m (10 ft) in a growing season, so needs regular pruning, and it will still produce flowers the same year as they flower on the current season's growth.

Pruning should be carried out from late winter to early spring to two or three buds of the previous season's wood. If needed they can have branches cut right back to ground level and will respond with new strong growth, which can be retrained to fill any open areas.
ASPECT: Full sun.
FLOWERING: July – September.
HARDINESS: -5 to -10 °C (23 to 14 °F).

6–12 m (20–39 ft)

3–5 m (10–16 ft)

OPPOSITE
Trachelospermum jasminoides

PREVIOUS PAGE
Campsis radicans – stunning trusses of large trumpet-like flowers

CLEMATIS CIRRHOSA
Winter clematis
RANUNCULACEAE

A semi-evergreen climbing shrub that will keep its leaves all year round, except for the coldest winters, when they will soon grow back in spring. They are glossy and quite variable, and can be entire or divided, or both on the same plant. The hanging, bell-shaped flowers are cream or pale yellow, and occasionally speckled or spotted on their inside. Like many climbers that are not self-clinging it is ideal for training over pergolas, along fences and other structures.

It's a great plant for any bees that venture out during mild spells in late winter and early spring, as a source of food.

Clematis cirrhosa should be grown where you will be able to appreciate it when it's at its best, during the colder months of the year. I grow a plant outside my kitchen window. It has never been watered since its first season, and is now six years old. It continues to flower profusely, and brightens dull winters days for me every time it catches my eye. Even when the flowers are over the silky seed heads are every bit as attractive as the flowers and will continue to delight.

The one downside to this climber is that it does look a bit untidy during the summer when most of its leaves are discoloured.

Winter-flowering clematis should be pruned after flowering, which will encourage further flowering. They can be left longer so you can enjoy the seed heads, but prune before new growth starts.

ASPECT: Full sun to partial shade.
FLOWERING: November – March.
HARDINESS: -5 to -10 °C (23 to 14 °F).

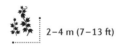 2–4 m (7–13 ft)

2–6 m (7–20 ft)

CLEMATIS FLAMMULA
Fragrant clematis
RANUNCULACEAE

This is a strong-growing deciduous climber that forms into a dense maze of woody stems. These are clothed with glossy green bipinnate leaves divided into leaflets, usually in threes. The pure white, fragrant, four-petalled flowers are centred with numerous creamy stamens, and are produced in abundance in loose clusters over the whole plant. The flowers are followed by attractive pompom-like silky seed heads.

Pruning should be done regularly to avoid this clematis becoming too tangled. Prune in late winter or early spring before new growth starts as it flowers in late summer on growth made the same season.

ASPECT: Full sun to partial shade.
FLOWERING: July – September.
HARDINESS: -10 to -15 °C (14 to 5 °F).

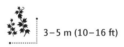 3–5 m (10–16 ft)

2–6 m (7–20 ft)

Producing masses of sweet, almond-scented flowers in midsummer

Clematis flammula

LONICERA ETRUSCA 'SUPERBA'
Etruscan honeysuckle
CAPRIFOLIACEAE

A deciduous, sometimes semi-evergreen woody climber that needs some support for its twining stems to grow up. The long twining stems have glaucous-green leaves, which are fused at the base encircling the stem.

Trained on trellis in a courtyard, this climber will fill the area with evening fragrance from the abundant flowers, which are arranged in circular clusters. The white flowers open with hints of reddish-pink, turning a more apricot yellow as they mature, and have long, protruding stamens, followed by bright red, rounded berries. It requires a sunny spot in the garden to do well.

ASPECT: Full sun.

FLOWERING: April – July.

HARDINESS: -10 to -15 °C (14 to 5 °F).

2–4 m (7–13 ft)

1.5–2.5 m (5–8 ft)

PARTHENOCISSUS TRICUSPIDATA
Boston ivy
VITACEAE

Boston ivy is another confusing common name as this plant is not related to ivy and is native to Asia! Its other common name of Japanese creeper is much more apt.

It is a deciduous, woody, self-clinging climber that will vigorously cover walls or fences. Because of the way the sticky pads on the ends of the tendrils attach themselves they do not penetrate the surface, and so in themselves are not damaging. But if the surface they are allowed to grow on is not sound, then removal of the plant may cause some damage.

The specific epithet *tricuspidata* refers to the three-lobed leaves, which are bright green in the spring and early summer but transform to give a spectacular display of

Lonicera etrusca **'Superba'**

fiery reds in autumn. There probably isn't anything that can match them for sheer scale and colour.

The Herbarium building at Kew, which houses the largest collection of dried plant specimens in the world, has one on its wall on the western side of the building from the bottom to top. It is a full 10 m (33 ft) high, even though its roots are restricted by the building's footings on one side, and heavily used paving on its other. It survived droughts in the 1970s and 1980s and others more recently, and continues to put on an amazing show year after year.

During early development it will need some support until it establishes, and also checking to ensure it doesn't grow into unwanted areas.

ASPECT: Full sun or partial shade.

FLOWERING: June – August, inconspicuous.

HARDINESS: -10 to -15 °C (14 to 5 °F).

5–20 m (16–66 ft)

5–10 m (16-33 ft)

ROSA SEMPERVIRENS
Mediterranean evergreen rose
ROSACEAE

This pretty climbing and scrambling rose is an evergreen shrub in all but the coldest of winters, when it will shed some of its leaves or they will brown and shrivel, growing back the following year. The name *sempervirens* means 'lives forever', or evergreen. It has long arching stems, with sparse backward-curving thorns. The glossy leaves shine when lit up by the sun. The four-petalled flowers are slightly fragrant, and are borne in terminal clusters, of up to seven individuals, becoming almost flat when fully open, displaying their large central boss of prominent orange stamens. The flowers are followed by small, oval, orange-red hips.

ASPECT: Full sun.

FLOWERING: July – September.

HARDINESS: 0 to -5 °C (32 to 23 °F).

4–6 m (13–20 ft)

3–5 m (10–16 ft)

Rosa sempervirens

SOLANUM CRISPUM 'GLASNEVIN'
Chilean potato vine
SOLANACEAE

This is a large, vigorous, scrambling semi-evergreen climber that is perfect for covering a sunny fence or wall, and will do equally well grown through other plants on a pergola. It will need some training and tying in to wires or a trellis. This is the hardiest of the species, and 'Glasnevin' produces the most prolific quantity of flowers over a long period. The exotic-looking clusters of fragrant flowers are purple or lilac, with a pronounced pointed, yellow centre.

Being semi-deciduous it will lose some of its leaves in the winter, and in the coldest areas will lose all the leaves, but new foliage will reappear in spring. Like most climbers it can become a bit bare around the base. Planting low-growing shrubs disguises this and improves their appearance.

Any pruning should be carried out in spring before new growth develops, and not after flowering as with hardier climbers, because any new young growth produced late in the year will suffer badly in early frosts. Pruning to maintain a tidy habit and to a framework is all that is required. It can be cut back hard if necessary to encourage a more bushy habit.

ASPECT: Full sun.
FLOWERING: June – September.
HARDINESS: -5 to -10 °C (23 to 14 °F).

2–6 m (7–20 ft)

1–5 m (3–16 ft)

Late flowering climber at its best when many other flowers have passed their peak

Solanum crispum 'Glasnevin'

TRACHELOSPERMUM JASMINOIDES
Star jasmine
APOCYNACEAE

A woody, evergreen climber that needs some support for its long twining stems to grow through. Trellises, a pergola or an arch are ideal. Alternatively grow it in a large pot or container, either up a support or trailing over the sides.

The leaves are oval-shaped and dark, glossy green for most of the year, but turn a lovely bronze or deep red colour in the autumn and winter.

The pure white, star-shaped flowers are produced from midsummer, and are borne in clusters. They remind me of small, white propellers in the way each of the five petals is almost at right angles to the adjacent one and twisting from the centre. The flowers have a strong, rich perfume.

The best spot to grow *Trachelospermum* is against a warm, sunny wall, where it will thrive and flower well all summer. In a patio or courtyard garden a close seating area will be rewarded by its superb fragrance. It is fairly slow-growing, which means it needs very little pruning to keep it in check.

ASPECT: Full sun or partial shade.
FLOWERING: June – August.
HARDINESS: -5 to -10 °C (23 to 14 °F).

4–8 m (13–26 ft)

4–8 m (13–26 ft)

VITIS COIGNETIAE
Crimson glory vine
VITACEAE

It is very hardy and drought-friendly, but you will need space to grow this stunning climber. A strong and vigorous deciduous climbing shrub, it attaches itself by tendrils, but needs supporting wires or a trellis and will cover an unsightly wall or fence quite quickly.

This ornamental climber from Japan is mainly grown for its impressive display of autumn colour. The large tri-lobed leaves with a heart-shaped base have deeply impressed veins and can get up to 30 cm (12 in) across. They are dark green during the summer months, but during autumn they transform into fiery shades of yellows and oranges, ending up a glorious bright crimson-red. It is reliable year after year. This vine also produces clusters of small, black inedible fruits.

Although this is a climber that will scramble up though a large tree to over 20 m (66 ft) if allowed, it can also be kept in check when regularly pruned. I have had one restricted on a 2.5 m (8 ft) high fence, allowing it to grow around 5 m (16 ft) along the fence.

Pruning must be done during the winter months, as like all vines it will bleed badly once growth has started in the spring. Later in the year this isn't such a problem if you need to trim a few odd bits.

ASPECT: Full sun or partial shade.
FLOWERING: May – June, insignificant.
HARDINESS: -10 to -15 °C (14 to 5 °F).

more than 15 m (49 ft)

2–5 m (7–16 ft)

WISTERIA SINENSIS
Chinese wisteria
FABACEAE

The flower power and scent of a mature Wisteria arguably cannot be bettered by any other climbing plant. It may not have the longest flowering season, but what a flowering season! Often seen as large plants adorning the fronts of houses with their roots growing close to the dry, and often limited soil available around the footings, they have no trouble dealing with these harsh conditions and perform year after year.

Wisteria sinensis is probably the most

Long, pendulous, bluish-lilac, scented flowers make Chinese wisteria a champion among climbing plants

Wisteria sinensis

popular of the wisterias. It is a deciduous climbing shrub, and a noble plant indeed. It produces long, vigorous, twining stems, which all twine in an anticlockwise direction (curiously the stems of Japanese wisterias, *Wisteria floribunda* twine in a clockwise direction). The stems need some support, wires if grown as a wall shrub. The new leaves are produced just as the flowers open, and are initially bronze, unfurling to a pale yellow-green colour, which contrasts well with the long, hanging racemes of pea-like flowers. The lilac-blue flowers are sweetly scented, and each drooping raceme can be over 30 cm (12 in) long.

Pruning should be done twice a year. The main pruning is done during their dormant period, cutting lateral shoots back to two or three buds from the main stem, and during summer, long wispy growths cut back to five or six buds, to keep them tidy.

Wisterias are most commonly bought as grafted plants, which flower much earlier than those produced from cuttings or seed.

There is also a white form, *Wisteria sinensis* 'Alba', as well as many cultivars.
ASPECT: Full sun or partial shade.
FLOWERING: May – June.
HARDINESS: -15 to -20 °C (5 to -4 °F).

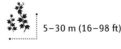

5–30 m (16–98 ft)

5–10 m (16–33 ft)

Grasses

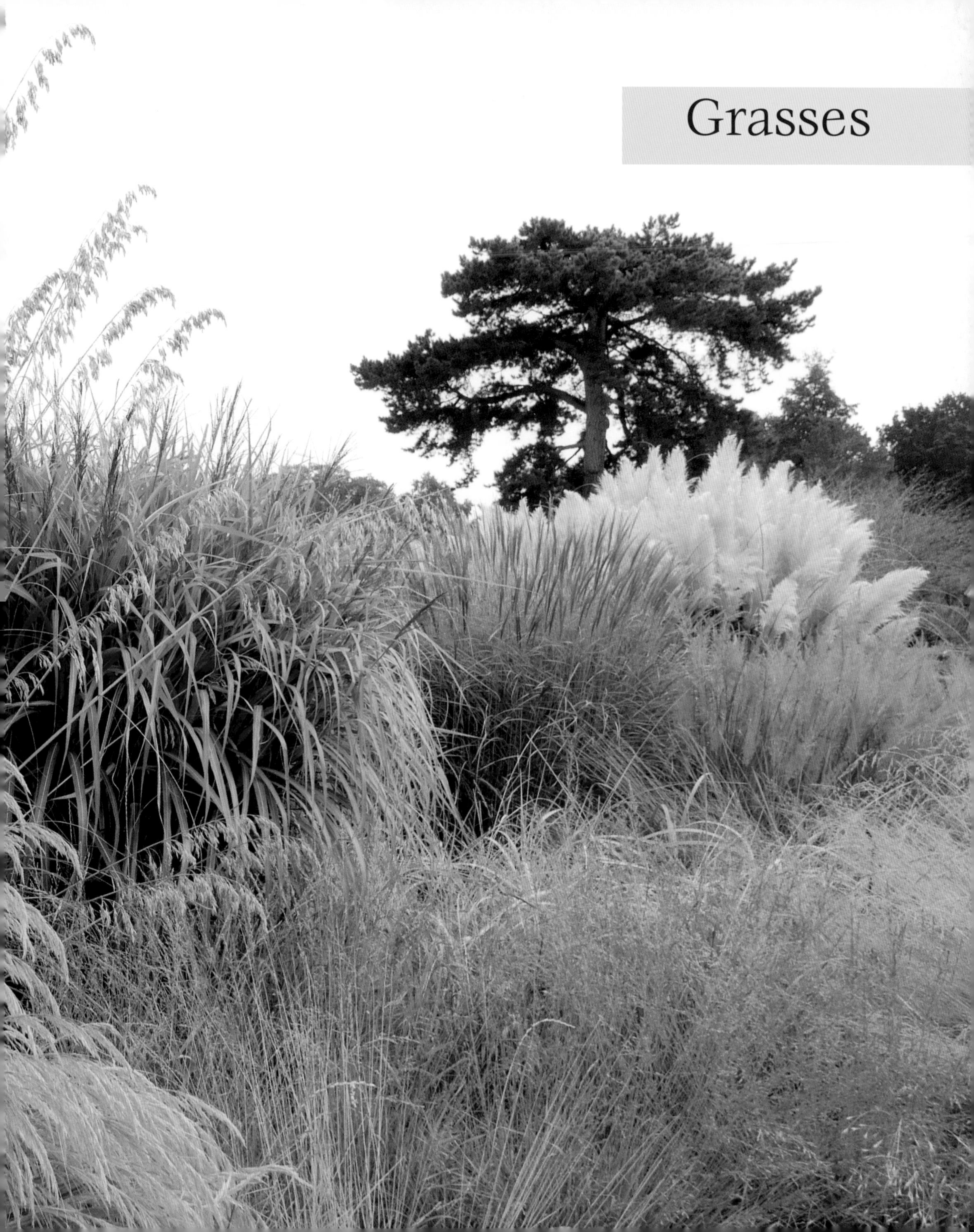

BRIZA MEDIA
Quaking grass
POACEAE

A semi-evergreen and short-lived perennial, this is a pretty ornamental grass that is definitely worth growing. Individual plants form tight clumps of grey-green leaves from which tall stems of branched flowerheads are produced. It should be grown in groups to get the best effect. The delicate quaking flowerheads turn straw-coloured when ripe, taking only the slightest of breezes for them to shake and sway.

It should be cut back hard in spring if the clumps become untidy.

As with many grasses, it is excellent for drying.

Briza media 'Russells' is a taller variegated form to around 1 m (3 ft) tall, with a white edge to the leaves.

ASPECT: Full sun or partial shade.
FLOWERING: May – August.
HARDINESS: -5 to -10 °C (23 to 14 °F).

 50–80 cm (20–32 in)

10–30 cm (4–12 in)

CALAMAGROSTIS × ACUTIFLORA 'KARL FOERSTER'
Feather reed grass
POACEAE

Stiff upright stems are a feature of this tall, architectural, clump-forming grass. The bright green erect stems and wide strap-like leaves contrast well with their feathery flowering spikes, which start off green, before taking on a purplish tone, and then both the stems and the flowerheads turn straw-coloured late in the season, remaining attractive throughout the winter. This gives them great all year-round interest.

Very easy to maintain, they need to be cut down to ground level in February, just before the new growth starts. It is one of the earliest grasses, producing new shoots in early March.

ASPECT: Full sun or partial shade.
FLOWERING: July – September.
HARDINESS: -5 to -10 °C (23 to 14 °F).

 1–1.5 m (3–5 ft)

50–75 cm (20–30 in)

Calamagrostis × acutiflora 'Karl Foerster'

PREVIOUS PAGE
Grasses give year-round interest in form and colour

FESTUCA GLAUCA 'ELIJAH BLUE'
Blue fescue
POACEAE

A small mound-forming grass, producing tussocks of blue needle-like leaves. In summer bluish-green flower spikes are produced, turning straw-coloured as they mature. But it is a plant that is really grown for its steely-blue foliage and needs to be in full sun to really perform and bring out its best colour. Very effective when grown in gravel, drifting through taller plants. Its dwarf nature also makes it an ideal grass for a rock garden. Remove any dead foliage in winter as the plants can become a bit scruffy-looking.

No pruning required.

ASPECT: Full sun.
FLOWERING: June – July.
HARDINESS: -10 to -15 °C (14 to 5 °F).

 20–30 cm (8–12 in)

20–30 cm (8–12 in)

LAGURUS OVATUS
Bunny's tail grass
POACEAE

A very pretty little hardy annual grass from the Mediterranean, where it is often seen growing along roadside verges, in the field margins of olive groves and in open, sunny, woodland glades.

It is quite obvious where it gets its common name from, and is also called hare's tail grass. The fluffy flowering seed heads are green, turning white as they mature. Being hardy it will self-seed each year, but never becomes unruly, producing nice tidy clumps.

Makes a great cut plant, with the dried stems lasting indefinitely.

ASPECT: Full sun.
FLOWERING: September – October.
HARDINESS: -5 to -10 °C (23 to 14 °F).

Festuca glauca **'Elijah Blue'**

Lagurus ovatus

 10–50 cm (4–20 in)

10–50 cm (4–20 in)

MISCANTHUS SINENSIS 'FERNER OSTEN'
Chinese silver grass
POACEAE

The cultivar name 'Ferner Osten' translated from German literally means 'Far East', alluding to the fact that this grass species originates from Asia. There are many cultivars of *Miscanthus sinensis* but I like this one particularly for its upright stature and clump-forming nature. The open, branching flowering plumes turn a warm coppery-red colour in autumn, before fading to silver. The leaves also have an attractive red tint to them during autumn.

Stems should be left over winter as, as with many grasses, the stems continue to be attractive, particularly when frosted. Cut back to ground level in spring.

ASPECT: Full sun.
FLOWERING: September – October.
HARDINESS: -10 to -15 °C (14 to 5 °F).

 1–1.5 m (3–5 ft)

50–75 cm (20–30 in)

Miscanthus sinensis 'Ferner Osten'

MISCANTHUS SINENSIS 'ZEBRINUS'
Zebra grass

POACEAE

An unusual-looking grass, with creamy-yellow bands of colour at intervals along the leaf blades.

This perennial grass forms dense clumps of narrow green leaves with striking lighter horizontal bands, making an unusual form of variegation that is quite different from other grasses. It is an exceptional foliage plant, producing flowering spikes in autumn. It is an old cultivar and was a favourite plant used by the influential plantswoman and garden designer Gertrude Jekyll.

It should be cut back hard in January before the new leaves start to appear. As well as growing in a bed or border *Miscanthus sinensis* 'Zebrinus' makes a great container-grown plant.

ASPECT: Full sun.

FLOWERING: September – October.

HARDINESS: -10 to -15 °C (14 to 5 °F).

 1–1.5 m (3–5 ft)

75 cm–1.5 m (30 in–5 ft)

Miscanthus sinensis 'Zebrinus'

NASSELLA TENUISSIMA
Mexican feather grass

POACEAE

Previously known as *Stipa tenuissima*. There are so many grasses that it is difficult to choose between them as many are garden-worthy, but I have picked this one as I think it is the most versatile, being medium in size and deciduous. This makes it quick to flower each season, forming small clumps with hair-like blooms.

Each spring new, fine, yellow-green growth appears, and produces a fountain of arching leaves, which sway in the slightest of breezes, softening the areas between other plants. From early summer feathery silver flowerheads form, and as the season progresses these mature to a golden brown.

Great in a gravel garden, or border, it is also a good grass to grow in a large container for a patio or sunny courtyard.

This is a grass that will self-seed, but the seedlings are easily removed.

ASPECT: Full sun.

FLOWERING: June – September.

HARDINESS: -5 to -10 °C (23 to 14 °F).

 40–60 cm (16–24 in)

10–50 cm (4–20 in)

PANICUM VIRGATUM 'HEAVY METAL'
Switch grass
POACEAE

An ornamental deciduous grass, native
to the prairies of America and Canada,
it dies back below ground level each
winter, reappearing the following spring.
It produces tall, upright clumps, which
are slowly spread by their rhizomes. The
blue-grey leafy stems are very metallic in
colour, during spring and summer, when
it produces inflorescences of purple-pink
flowers, and then in autumn the stems
turn a yellow-brown, retaining the seed
heads.

ASPECT: Full sun.

FLOWERING: August – September.

HARDINESS: -10 to -15 °C (14 to 5 °F).

 50 cm–1 m (20 in–3 ft)

50–75 cm (20–30 in)

PENNISETUM ALOPECUROIDES
Fountain grass
POACEAE

Fountain grasses are clump-forming
perennials and make highly decorative
ornamental grasses. They have neat,
tidy green foliage, erect in the centre
and arching around the outer edges of
the clumps. During late summer they
really come in to their own when the
flowerheads appear, dozens in each
clump, looking like bushy pink squirrels'
tails.

Like most grasses fountain grasses
turn a rich bronze colour during autumn
and remain attractive right through
the winter, holding on to their pretty
flowerheads.

ASPECT: Full sun.

FLOWERING: July – September.

HARDINESS: 0 to -5 °C (32 to 23 °F).

 50 cm–1.2 m (20 in–4 ft)

50–80 cm (20–32 in)

Nassella tenuissima

Palms

BUTIA CAPITATA
Jelly palm
ARECACEAE

One of the hardiest feather palms, this is really for the plant enthusiast as there are hardier palms, such as *Chamaerops* (see below), *Cordyline* (see right) and *Trachycarpus* (page 61). But given a sunny, sheltered spot out of the coldest winds it should survive and do well. As the palm trunk thickens with age so will its hardiness increase. The silvery-grey feather-like leaves give this palm a very graceful appearance. Lightly prune, cutting any damaged fronds back to their base in spring.

It is well suited to and will also happily grow in large containers, in a free-draining soil mix, making it ideal for courtyard and patio gardens.

Apparently, mature plants during a hot summer can produce large edible fruits that are ideal for making jams and jellies.

Apart from removing dead or damaged leaves no other pruning is necessary.

ASPECT: Full sun to partial shade.
FLOWERING: July – September.
HARDINESS: Should be hardy to around -10 °C (14 °F).

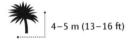
4–5 m (13–16 ft)

2.5–3 m (8–10 ft)

CHAMAEROPS HUMILIS
Dwarf fan palm
ARECACEAE

Definitely a must-have plant, and one that can be used in many different growing situations. Great in a gravel garden, courtyard or on a patio in a large pot or container, this is a tough and drought-friendly plant. In the wild it is generally found growing in poor rocky soils in the full Mediterranean sun.

PREVIOUS PAGE
Drought tolerant palms create a tropical look in gardens

Chamaerops humilis

This small palm gives big impact, with large palmate leaves divided into 20–30 deeply cut, stiff segments. The leaves are held on long spiny petioles. Generally, the plants are quite short, producing stemless hummocks, but with age they grow short fibrous single or multi-stemmed trunks.

Mature plants produce dense clusters of small creamy-yellow flowers in late spring, and these develop into brown, inedible date-like fruits.

The removal of dead or damaged leaves is all that is required.

ASPECT: Full sun to partial shade.
FLOWERING: April – June.
HARDINESS: -5 to -10 °C (23 to 14 °F).

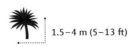
1.5–4 m (5–13 ft)

1–2 m (3–7 ft)

CORDYLINE AUSTRALIS
Cabbage palm
ASPARAGACEAE

Originally from New Zealand, this palm-like tree most commonly forms a single trunk but can also be multi-stemmed.

It has a branching crown, with stiff, sword-like leaves, produced terminally on the branches. When these plants are mature, they will have plumes of tiny, fragrant, creamy-white flowers, followed by small, round, white berries with a blue tint.

As well as being drought-tolerant, *Cordyline australis* is also tolerant of wind and salt spray, and is a very popular coastal plant commonly planted in south-west England. Young plants make good container plants for conservatories, patios and courtyards.

There is also a less common darker-leaved form, *Cordyline australis* 'Atropurpurea', and while the name might suggest that the leaves are purple, they are in fact brownish.

Pruning is very easy, with no cutting required: just remove dying lower leaves by pulling them off with a downward motion. The spent flower stalk does, though, need to be removed with loppers, cutting as low down in the rosette as you can manage.

ASPECT: Full sun to partial shade.
FLOWERING: July – August.
HARDINESS: 0 to -5 °C (32 to 23 °F).

4–6 m (13–20 ft)

2–3 m (7–10 ft)

PHOENIX CANARIENSIS
Canary island date palm
ARECACEAE

A great plant to give a tropical feel to a garden or patio, with its large frond-like leaves. But it is really only suited to the warmer, frost-protected areas of the UK. It will tolerate a bit of frost, but not

TRACHYCARPUS FORTUNEI
Chusan palm
ARECACEAE

If you want something that will give a tropical and exotic feel to your garden, whether in a container or in the ground, that is outstandingly hardy, then this is the plant that will not fail you.

Trachycarpus fortunei is a palm native to China that has been grown in the UK since the mid-nineteenth century. It is relatively fast-growing, with a single, fibrous trunk, clothed in the remains of the old leaf bases, looking like straw matting. The huge fan-like leaves are all produced at the top of the trunk, on long, stiff petioles, and can be over 1 m (3 ft) wide, made up of many small leaflets. In late summer *Trachycarpus* produces arching clusters of pale-yellow flowers, which add to the exotic feel of this palm.

Trachycarpus wagnerianus is very similar to *T. fortunei* but has a shorter trunk and smaller leaves, so may be more suitable for smaller areas, where space might be an issue.

Although *Trachycarpus* is fully hardy and drought-tolerant, it is best grown in a sheltered spot away from strong winds, as the leaves can look tatty from a battering of wind.

ASPECT: Full sun or partial shade.
FLOWERING: August – September.
HARDINESS: -5 to -10 °C (23 to 14 °F).

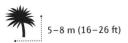

5–8 m (16–26 ft)

2–3 m (7–10 ft)

Cordyline australis

for prolonged periods, and not hard, penetrating frosts. Planted in a courtyard garden or in a large container it should be fine.

In areas that are relatively frost-free, this palm forms a trunk and will grow fairly quickly. In central London and some coastal areas, it definitely makes a feature, whether in a large tub or as a larger specimen growing in a sheltered

garden, and I hope is a plant that will become more commonly planted.

ASPECT: Full sun, in a sheltered position.
FLOWERING: May – June.
HARDINESS: 0 to -5 °C (32 to 23 °F).

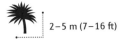

2–5 m (7–16 ft)

2–5 m (7–16 ft)

CALAMINTHA NEPETA
Lesser catmint
LAMIACEAE

This small perennial gives lots of value. Its compact, bushy form makes it ideal for the front of a border. The grey-green leaves are very aromatic, with a minty fragrance when crushed or brushed against, and the whole plant is covered in clouds of lavender flowers throughout the summer, lasting usually until the first frosts. It is semi-evergreen, keeping its leaves in mild winters.

Calamintha also does well in a container, and is a plant loved by bees and butterflies.

Cutting back in autumn after flowering is all that is required to tidy old growth. New growth will appear the following spring.

ASPECT: Full sun.
FLOWERING: July – September.
HARDINESS: -10 to -15 °C (14 to 5 °F).

20–50 cm (8–20 in)

20–50 cm (8–20 in)

CENTRANTHUS RUBER
Red valerian
CAPRIFOLIACEAE

This pretty perennial has tall stems of bluish-green leaves and foaming heads of pink or crimson flowers. It is an ideal plant for growing in wilder parts of a garden, a wildflower area or in the gravel garden where its variable colours will come to life.

When happy it will freely seed around, but is easily weeded out from areas where it's not wanted. It looks good when left to find its own niche, especially in the cracks and gaps in paving and low walls. *Centranthus ruber* and its white form have naturalised themselves in many parts of southern England, especially around coastal areas.

Cut down stems in autumn after flowering.

ASPECT: Full sun to partial shade.
FLOWERING: June – October.
HARDINESS: -10 to -15 °C (14 to 5 °F).

50 cm–1 m (20 in–3 ft)

10–50 cm (4–20 in)

Centranthus ruber

Cerastium tomentosum

CERASTIUM TOMENTOSUM
Dusty miller
CARYOPHYLLACEAE

This is a great little ground cover plant producing carpets of small, white flowers, which are carried above woolly, silver, evergreen foliage. The epithet *tomentosum* means covered with dense, short hairs, and these hairs cover the stems as well. *Cerastium tomentosum* is a perennial plant that really enjoys a sunny spot (originating in alpine zones) where it will spread fairly quickly and looks particularly good spilling over rocks and containers. The five-petalled flowers are produced profusely over a fairly long period, from late spring and through the summer.

It is a fast-spreading plant by virtue of its rhizomes but is easily controlled by dividing in spring or autumn, and it can be cut back hard to around 2.5 cm (1 in) after flowering to keep it in check and tidy. This will also prevent it self-seeding into unwanted areas of the garden.

ASPECT: Full sun.
FLOWERING: May – August.
HARDINESS: -15 to -20 °C (5 to -4 °F).

10–30 cm (4–12 in)

75 cm–1 m (30 in–3 ft)

Crambe maritima

CRAMBE MARITIMA
Sea kale
BRASSICACEAE

This plant is native to the UK and Europe, growing wild in the shingle along parts of the coastline.

It forms large clumps, bearing large, thick, waxy, grey-green leaves with deep, wavy margins. The young leaves have a purple tinge to them and purple stems. During early summer, large clusters of honey-scented, white, four-petalled flowers are produced. *Crambe maritima* looks particularly good grown in honey-coloured gravel, which really shows off its grey-green foliage. The young stems of this sea kale are also edible, collected in spring and steamed.

Cutting back to ground level in autumn will tidy away the dead and dying old leaves before the new season's growth.

ASPECT: Full sun to partial shade.
FLOWERING: May – July.
HARDINESS: -15 to -20 °C (5 to -4 °F).

 50–75 cm (20–30 in)

20–50 cm (8–20 in)

DIANELLA TASMANICA
Tasmanian flax lily
XANTHORRHOEACEAE

An evergreen grass-like perennial, with large strap-shaped leaves, which grows in clumps.

During early summer it produces branched flower spikes, with violet-blue, star-shaped flowers and showy yellow anthers that protrude with age as the flower petals become reflexed. The flowers are followed by large, dark blue, shiny berries, which persist into the winter.

No real pruning is necessary, but divide large clumps in mid-spring.

ASPECT: Full sun to partial shade.
FLOWERING: May – June.
HARDINESS: 0 to -5 °C (32 to 23 °F).

 50 cm–1 m (20 in–3 ft)

10–50 cm (4–20 in)

DIGITALIS OBSCURA
Sunset foxglove
PLANTAGINACEAE

Foxgloves are usually better known as woodland plants, but *Digitalis obscura* is a sun-loving foxglove that in the wild grows along open mountain tracks and hillsides in full sun. It will, like other foxgloves, be quite happy in some shade.

A tall perennial with glaucous, linear, lance-shaped, sessile leaves that turn down at their tips. The flowers grow along one-sided, tall flower spikes, with flowers opening from the bottom up. They are in variable colours of brownish-orange, tubular in shape, with red veins and spotting inside and a darker, hairy margin.

Another common name for them is the rusty foxglove, because of their colouration.

ASPECT: Full sun to partial shade.
FLOWERING: April – July.
HARDINESS: 0 to -5 °C (32 to 23 °F).

 10–50 cm (4–20 in)

10–30 cm (4–12 in)

Digitalis obscura

OPPOSITE *Euphorbia seguieriana* (see page 75)

Echinops ritro

ECHINOPS RITRO
Globe thistle
ASTERACEAE

This is a clump-forming hardy perennial with leaves that are dark, silver-green above with soft, white hairs below. The stiff leaves are deeply divided with spiny margins and form a low mound from which tall, stiff, hairy branched stems rise, each terminating in perfectly round, pompom-like flowerheads, which are spiky and dark blue at first, opening to reveal small star-like flowers, becoming a paler blue. There are probably few other flowers that will attract as many pollinators as the globe thistle. Bees and butterflies literally cover the whole flowerhead. The globe thistle also makes a great cut flower.

'Veitch's Blue' – is a darker blue cultivar.

Echinops bannaticus 'Taplow Blue' – is the best-known cultivar of this species and produces bright, metallic-blue, spherical flowerheads around 5 cm (2 in) in diameter, on long silvery stems with glaucous, prickly edged leaves. It eventually produces architectural clumps that go well with golden grasses like *Miscanthus*. It also makes an excellent cut flower.

The name *Echinops* comes from the Greek *echinos*, meaning hedgehog and *opsis*, meaning appearance; another common name for this plant is the hedgehog thistle.

Deadhead plants after flowering to prevent self-seeding, and divide if needed in spring or autumn.

ASPECT: Full sun to partial shade.
FLOWERING: July – August.
HARDINESS: -15 to -20 °C (5 to -4 °F).

 50 cm–1 m (20 in–3 ft)

10–50 cm (4–20 in)

ERIGERON KARVINSKIANUS
Mexican fleabane
ASTERACEAE

This is a small woody perennial that produces masses of small, daisy-like flowers, which open white, becoming pink with age, and with yellow centres, all of which give this little plant a mix of colours the whole time it is in flower. Its small size disguises the fact that is a very tough character. It will seed itself around into walls, paving and anywhere it can find good drainage. And this I think adds to its charm. It is great in pots on patios and in courtyard gardens, looks at home growing in gravel, spilling over walls, in rock gardens or at the front of a border. A truly versatile little plant that's loved by bees and butterflies as well.

ASPECT: Full sun.
FLOWERING: June – October.
HARDINESS: -10 to -15 °C (14 to 5 °F).

 10–20 cm (4–8 in)

10–50 cm (4–20 in)

ESCHSCHOLZIA CALIFORNICA
Californian poppy
PAPAVERACEAE

The Californian poppy is a short-lived perennial, often treated as an annual, as it sets seed so readily, producing new plants within its own growing season. The bluish-green foliage is fern-like, and contrasts well with the brilliant orange, single, deep-cupped flowers. The flowers open with the morning sun, closing for the night. Seeding itself around produces differing shades of orange. Removing the long, curved seed pods lengthens the flowering period and reduces any unwanted seedlings.

Grown en masse this plant looks amazing, but even if you only have room for a few plants it is well worth growing for the joy it gives. It's a plant that always brightens my day.

The orange colour of these poppies and the bluish-purple of lavenders are a great combination. It also works well with straw-coloured golden grasses like stipas in dry gravel.

ASPECT: Full sun.
FLOWERING: May – July.
HARDINESS: 0 to -5 °C (32 to 23 °F).

 10–30 cm (4–12 in)

10–15 cm (4–6 in)

Eschscholzia californica

ERYNGIUM
Eryngo or sea holly
APIACEAE

Eryngium is a large genus, with 230 different species, including annuals, biennials and perennials, and dozens of cultivars, giving lots of choices when planning a planting scheme. Here are just a few that might make selection a little easier. The one thing they all have in common is their showy, spiny bracts below the flowers, making them very distinctive. They look good planted in small groups, particularly in gravel.

ERYNGIUM AGAVIFOLIUM – is a statuesque plant and very different from most other eryngiums. It is an evergreen perennial that can grow very tall. The leaves are distinctive too, long, sword-like, succulent-looking and pale-green, with spiny margins form a basal rosette. The leaves also grow along the length of the tall, branched flower spike. The flowers are small, greenish-white, held in thimble-shaped heads. Height 1.5 m (5 ft) × spread 1 m (3 ft).

ERYNGIUM ALPINUM – has steel blue flowers on long stems, which are surrounded by a ring of upright fine-cut, feathery, floral bracts, making this herbaceous perennial quite distinctive. Height 50–75 cm (20–30 in) × spread 10–30 cm (4–12 in).

ERYNGIUM BOURGATII – is a cultivar with outstanding violet-blue flower bracts. It was grown from seed collected from plants growing in the Picos de Europa mountains in northern Spain. The foliage is spiny, slightly variegated and multi-stemmed. The showy bracts open silver-grey and turn blue as the flowers mature.

The striking spiky foliage and bracts combine well with a haze of *Verbena bonariensis*

Eryngium bourgatii 'Picos Amethyst'

Height 40–60 cm (16–24 in) × spread 40–60 cm (16–24 in).

ERYNGIUM GIGANTEUM – named after the nineteenth-century gardener Ellen Willmott, who supposedly would secretly scatter the seeds of this plant in other people's gardens. It is a herbaceous perennial, with marbled, heart-shaped basal leaves, and spiny-toothed leaves growing up its thick, silver-green, branched stem. The large thimble-like flower (10 cm (4 in) long) is surrounded by a ruff of silver-grey bracts. Height 60 cm–1 m (24 in–3 ft) × spread 20–40 cm (8–16 in).

ERYNGIUM VARIIFOLIUM – has dark-green, glossy foliage heavily marbled with white-veined variegation, and is evergreen, so looks good all year round, and particularly during the winter months. Flowers are borne on branching stems, above long spiny bracts. It is more compact than most eryngiums, so one for a restricted growing space. Height 40 cm (16 in) × spread 20 cm (8 in).

ERYNGIUM YUCCIFOLIUM – is a tall evergreen perennial to around 1 m (3 ft) tall, with blue-green, sword-shaped leaves that have a spiny margin. The tall, branched stems produce clusters of small, rounded heads of whitish flowers in late summer, which like all eryngiums are very attractive to insects, particularly bees. Height 50 cm–1 m (20 in–3 ft) × spread 20–50 cm (8–20 in).

ERYNGIUM × ZABELII – was from an original cross between *E. alpinum* and *E. bourgatii*. This particular cultivar has blue stems, with finely toothed yellow foliage, and the bracts that surround the terminal flowers are blue at their base and have golden tips. Commonly known as the golden-leaved sea holly. Height 30–50 cm (12–20 in) × spread 30–40 cm (12–16 in).

The attractive flower stems can be left on over winter and cut back before new growth starts in spring.
ASPECT: Full sun.
FLOWERING: June – September.
HARDINESS: -10 to -15 °C (14 to 5 °F).

 Indicated individually

Indicated individually

EUPHORBIA
Spurges
EUPHORBIACEAE

The spurges are a huge family with thousands of species. Many of them are succulents and not hardy. But there are lots that are hardy and very drought-tolerant, showy and highly garden-worthy. The flowers of this genus are known in botanical terms as *cyathium*, meaning small, cup-shaped structures containing a reduced female flower and several tiny male flowers each with a single stamen. One note of caution is that all euphorbias produce a thick, latex-like, milky-white sap that is poisonous when any part of the plant is broken or cut, and will cause severe discomfort if wiped into the eyes or ingested, and can be a skin irritant. Wearing gloves when working with euphorbias is advised.

EUPHORBIA AMYGDALOIDES VAR. ROBBIAE – is a medium-sized, evergreen, spreading perennial with dark green foliage, forming rosettes of glossy oblong leaves along its stems, and then, in late spring, much paler lime-green flowers that last right through the summer. Its suckering, spreading habit makes it a useful ground cover plant, particularly in drier, shadier areas, brightening up areas under trees. It naturally occurs in woodland, so will tolerate quite a bit of shade, hence its common name wood spurge. But I much prefer the common name 'Mrs Robb's Bonnet'. It will do equally as well in full sun. It does need to be kept in check in small areas, though, as it will take over. It also freely self-seeds and the seedlings will revert to the wild form,

Summer's sulphur-yellow flower bracts turn red and bronze in autumn

Euphorbia epithymoides

which is much darker. So, remove any seedlings with red stems to ensure you keep the variety *robbiae* true.
Height 40–60 cm (16–24 in) × spread 40–60 cm (16–24 in).

EUPHORBIA CHARACIAS – big, tall and handsome. This is a favourite plant of many people, whether in an herbaceous or mixed border, or as a standalone feature plant. It was described by an Edwardian garden designer as 'one of the grandest of plants', and I think most will find it hard to disagree. *Euphorbia characias* produces large clumps of tall stems over 1 m (39 in) in height, with blue-grey foliage, topped from March to May in huge heads of yellow-green flowers, with dark eyes. Each of the stems is biennial, producing flowers in the second year, so after flowering these stems should be cut back in autumn. It is native to the Mediterranean, found growing in dry, stony soils, making it a very drought-tolerant plant. A common subspecies is *wulfenii*, and there is a cultivar of this subspecies, 'John

Tomlinson', with large rounded heads of bright yellow-green flowers, which originated from Kew Gardens. There are many other cultivars, including variegated plants such as *Euphorbia characias* 'Glacier Blue'. Height 75 cm–1.5 m (30 in–5 ft) × spread 75 cm–1.5 m (30 in–5 ft).

EUPHORBIA EPITHYMOIDES – is in my opinion one of the best of the smaller euphorbias. A stand-out perennial, it forms rounded, bushy plants with amazing clusters of bright acid-yellow flowers, which contrast wonderfully with the darker green lower foliage. There is also an autumn bonus, when the foliage turns a lovely bronze colour. Height 40–50 cm (16–20 in) × spread 40–60 cm (16–24 in).

EUPHORBIA MELLIFERA – forms a large shrub-like plant, which can make a tree in its native Madeira and the Canaries, where it reaches heights of up to 15 m (49 ft). But in the UK, it usually makes large domed-shaped shrubs, with long, smooth, pale green leafless stems. The long, narrow leaves cluster in whorls at the ends of these stems and are very distinctive, being glossy green above with a pale green midrib, and a grey-green underside. During spring brownish flowers are produced and give off a honey-like scent. The species name *mellifera* means honey. It is certainly hardy in the south of England, where even after occasional damage from frosts below -5 °C (23 °F) and more, it will grow again from the base. Height 1–2 m (3–7 ft) × spread 1–2.5 m (3–8 ft).

EUPHORBIA MYRSINITES – has growth that is prostrate and semi-succulent. Its long trailing stems have glaucous, blue-grey leaves, each one with a pointed tip, arranged spirally and overlapping all along the stem, terminating in a cluster of small lime-green flowers in early spring. Once the flowers are over, the leafy stems keep this plant looking attractive all year. Being fairly small and

Euphorbia myrsinites

prostrate makes it an ideal plant for a rock garden or the front of a gravel garden. Height 10–20 cm (4–8 in) × spread 10–50 cm (4–20 in).

EUPHORBIA RIGIDA – is superficially similar to *Euphorbia myrsinites*, but it has an upright habit. The leaves are

narrower than those of *E. myrsinites*, and are arranged in the same way, in an overlapping spiral all along their stem and are the same glaucous, blue-green colour. During autumn and winter, the leaves turn an attractive purple-violet. I remember the first time I came across this plant in the mountains of southern Spain. I was on a seed-collecting trip in October and saw this little plant growing (at the time I thought dying) among the rocky scree. I guessed it was probably annual, or had succumbed to the scorching summer sun, but later found out this was natural at this time of year. Another good plant for a rock garden. Height 30–50 cm (12–20 in) × spread 40–60 cm (16–24 in).

EUPHORBIA SEGUIERIANA – is one of the medium-sized spurges, but starts flowering later than most, usually in June, and has striking deep red, almost mahogany-coloured stems, which are a contrast to the blue-green leaves and loose, long-stemmed clusters of sulphur-yellow flowers. Height 20–50 cm (8–20 in) × spread 20–40 cm (8–16 in).

Old flowering shoots should be cut back to ground level from late summer to autumn.

ASPECT: Full sun to partial shade.
FLOWERING: March – July.
HARDINESS: -5 to -10 °C (23 to 14 °F).

 Indicated individually

Indicated individually

Euphorbia characias

FERULA COMMUNIS
Giant fennel
APIACEAE

A strikingly architectural perennial plant, with an individual stem that can be as thick as a broom stick. Unlike its edible cousin, the common fennel (*Foeniculum vulgare*), this one is not scented or edible. Around the base of the plant is an airy mound of finely cut leaves, which have a delicate appearance, but it is tough and very drought-tolerant. From late spring the flower spike begins to emerge from within the mound of leaves, eventually to produce an enormous branched flowerhead. Each of the rounded clusters of flowers is as big as a fist and made up of many small bright yellow flowers that are highly attractive to bees. The hollow flower stem contains a pith that when dried has been used as tinder. It will slowly burn inside the hollow stem, enabling it to be transported from one place to another.

Remove tall flower spikes down to ground level after flowering.

ASPECT: Full sun.

FLOWERING: June – July.

HARDINESS: -5 to -10 °C (23 to 14 °F).

2–3 m (7–10 ft)

50 cm–1 m (20 in–3 ft)

FOENICULUM VULGARE
Common fennel
APIACEAE

The tall green stems of fennel, with their flat heads of tiny yellow flowers, are often seen growing along the roadsides in the Mediterranean. I always enjoy rubbing the fine, hair-like, aromatic foliage in my fingers when walking along these roadsides in the warm Mediterranean sunshine. Its delicate foliage makes it very ornamental, where its airy

OPPOSITE *Eryngium yuccifolium* (see page 73)

characteristics produce an almost hazy or misty appearance. It is a plant that looks great in a small group in a large border or as a single specimen in a gravel bed. A tall perennial that looks good and tastes good too!

The form *Foeniculum vulgare* 'Purpureum', known as the bronze fennel, has bronze-purple young foliage, becoming grey-green with age.

Fennel has been used a culinary and medicinal herb since Roman times.

No pruning is required.

ASPECT: Full sun.

FLOWERING: July – August.

HARDINESS: -10 to -15 °C (14 to 5 °F).

1–2.5 m (3–8 ft)

20–50 cm (8–20 in)

GAURA LINDHEIMERI
Beeblossom
ONAGRACEAE

Native to Mexico and Texas, *Gaura* is an unusual and very different-looking

Foeniculum vulgare

perennial that has long arching stems that will need a bit of space to spread out. It is very free-flowering, with white, four-petalled flowers produced all along the wispy stems over a long period during summer. When grown in a large swathe it gives a wonderful effect, swaying and dancing in the wind, looking particularly good grown with grasses, such as *Stipa gigantea* or *S. tenuissima*.

The cultivar 'Siskiyou Pink' has flowers that are rose-pink with white margins, while 'Whirling Butterflies' is white-flowering, opening from pink buds.

Leave cutting back the flowered stems until spring, and clumps that have become too large for their space should also be divided in spring.

ASPECT: Full sun.

FLOWERING: June – September.

HARDINESS: -5 to -10 °C (23 to 14 °F).

75cm–1 m (30 in–3 ft)

50–75 cm (20–30 in)

Gaura lindheimeri 'Whirling Butterflies'

GERANIUM
Cranesbills
GERANIACEAE

Cranesbills must not be confused with the tender geraniums that are used for summer bedding and hanging baskets, namely the pelargoniums, which are not hardy. True geraniums are perennials, and perfectly hardy. They are commonly known as cranesbills because of the shape of their seed capsules, which are long and beak-like.

Geraniums are plants that make ideal ground cover, featuring many flower colours, and many have fragrant foliage, with new cultivars being produced in their dozens each year. Most prefer full sun, but they will all take some shade, so are a versatile group of plants.

I have only chosen a few of the many hundreds available, ones that I know well that are tried and tested.

GERANIUM MACRORRHIZUM – is

Geraniums and eryngiums

Thriving even in dry shade, the intense blue flowers are short-lived, finishing blooming in late spring

Geranium malviflorum

a mat-forming, semi-evergreen perennial, which keeps its leaves throughout a mild winter, but loses them during prolonged cold periods, with fresh, new growth appearing again in spring. It spreads by long rhizomes, covering quite large areas, making it a great ground cover plant, which will tolerate dry shade under trees. Grows in full sun and has good red autumn colour.

The leaves are aromatic, with their flowers held on long stems in small clusters of saucer-shaped, individual pink flowers. There is also a white form.

GERANIUM MALVIFLORUM – has a relatively short flowering period, but its large blue flowers, with darker veining to each petal, borne in small terminal clusters, above deeply dissected leaves, are worth giving garden space to. It flowers early and then disappears, making room for other later flowering plants.

GERANIUM SANGUINEUM – is a spreading perennial that loves full sun but will also grow well in partial shade. It is fairly slow to spread, but does so by rhizomes, and forms low hummocks of deeply cut palmate leaves. These leaves are almost completely covered during flowering by beautiful, cup-shaped magenta-coloured flowers, with white centres, veined petals and violet stamens. Also available in a white form. This little geranium is a great front-of-border plant.

Removing old leaves and flower stems is all that is needed. They can be cut back hard with shears if they become too untidy or winter-damaged.

ASPECT: Full sun.
FLOWERING: May – September.
HARDINESS: -15 to -20 °C (5 to -4 °F).

10–50 cm (4–20 in)

10–50 cm (4–20 in)

OPPOSITE *Eryngium agavifolium* (see page 73)

Iberis gibraltarica

IBERIS GIBRALTARICA
Gibraltar candytuft
BRASSICACEAE

A great little plant for a rock garden, the Gibraltar candytuft is surprisingly tough. Listed as a perennial, it is actually an evergreen sub-shrub, as it has a woody base. It has a low-growing and spreading habit, with thick, linear leaves.

It is very free-flowering and produces large flowerheads up to 8 cm (3 in) across, made up of small florets. The flowers are mainly lilac in colour but also come in various shades from white to pink and lilac, and cover the whole plant. It is planted in the Mediterranean Garden at Kew in wall crevices where it produces a small floral cascade.

Very little pruning necessary, and removing the seed heads and some of the longer, straggly growth over rocks is all that is required.

ASPECT: Full sun.
FLOWERING: April – July.
HARDINESS: -5 to -10 °C (23 to 14 °F).

10–20 cm (4–8 in)

10–30 cm (4–12 in)

KNIPHOFIA
Red hot pokers
ASPHODELACEAE

The common names of red hot poker and torch lily are both very apt. *Kniphofia* is definitely a plant that will bring an exotic feel to any garden. The spectacular flowers come in a wide range of colours and sizes, from the palest yellows and greens through to the deepest oranges and reds.

Originating from South Africa, where they are visited by sunbirds for their nectar, in the UK they are very attractive to insects, particularly bees, which will completely disappear into the long tubular flowers to enjoy the nectar.

Ensure the rhizomes are not too deeply planted as they will rot off if they become too wet for prolonged periods, and during wet winters.

Cut back foliage to the base during late autumn/early winter. Plants should also be periodically divided in spring when they become overcrowded.

There are many cultivars and newly introduced plants like the dwarf poco series, with plants that are around 40 cm (16 in) tall and ideal for planting at the front of a border or in containers. Below is a selection of kniphofias in varying colours and in height order from approximately 75 cm (30 in) to the tallest at 2 m (7 ft).

KNIPHOFIA 'Lemon Popsicle' – one of the shorter kniphofias, with pure yellow buds and flowers that are individually held horizontally, becoming pendulous once open.

KNIPHOFIA 'Bees Lemon' – a beautiful bright yellow inflorescence,

> Grown in large or small groups, fiery red hot pokers make exotic plantings when mixed with grasses

Kniphofia triangularis

opening from pale green buds. It flowers late in the season and over several weeks.

KNIPHOFIA 'Ice Queen' – lime-green in bud, fading to a paler green and then opening to white, and flowering from mid to late summer.

KNIPHOFIA TRIANGULARIS – as a straight species it can be quite variable in colour and form. Mostly bright orange-red, flowering from late summer. There are many selections from this species, including the cultivar 'Light of the World'.

KNIPHOFIA 'Nobilis' – the largest of the kniphofias, tall and statuesque, able to reach 2 m (6.6 ft) in height, with large bright orange flowerheads that turn yellow as they open. Despite its height if grown as a group it shouldn't need staking.

ASPECT: Full sun.
FLOWERING: April – November.
HARDINESS: -5 to -10 °C (23 to 14 °F).

30 cm–2 m (12 in–7 ft)

20 cm–1 m (8 in–3 ft)

Kniphofia 'Nobilis'

Kniphofia 'Ice Queen'

Kniphofia 'Lemon Popsicle'

Libertia peregrinans

LIBERTIA PEREGRINANS
Gold stripe libertia
IRIDACEAE

An evergreen grass-like plant native to New Zealand, and related to the iris. This plant forms small clumps, and spreads by producing running stolons, which wander away giving rise to new plants around the original one. These increase the clump size, but not in an invasive way, and the young plants can be collected to be used in other areas if needed. The wide sword-like leaves have a central orange vein, giving them a golden-orange glow, which intensifies in late summer. Among the leaves small white flowers appear in loose terminal clusters, opening in succession from early to mid summer. Plant at the edge of a border, gravel garden or in a container, to add architectural texture and colour.

ASPECT: Full sun or partial shade.
FLOWERING: June – July.
HARDINESS: -5 to -10 °C (23 to 14 °F).

 30–50 cm (12–20 in)

20–50 cm (8–20 in)

LIRIOPE MUSCARI
Big blue lily-turf
ASPARAGACEAE

This is a common little perennial that often gets overlooked but is highly versatile and will fit into many niches, tolerating a wide range of conditions is as tough as old boots. It is fine in full sun and drought to shade and wet soils, but prefers something in between.

The small, dark green, arching, strap-like leaves produce year-round interest, and then during autumn and into early winter, when most other flowers are over, this little lily produces a flowering stem from within its dense grass-like foliage of deep violet, bell-like flowers clustered along a short spike. If the leaves become a bit tatty and tired-looking, they

Liriope muscari

can be cut right down to the ground, rejuvenating the whole plant.

There is also a pretty white cultivar called *Liriope muscari* 'Monroe White' that would look good mixed in with the purple one.

ASPECT: Partial shade to full sun.
FLOWERING: August – November.
HARDINESS: -5 to -10 °C (23 to 14 °F).

 10–30 cm (4–12 in)

10–45 cm (4–18 in)

NEPETA × FAASENII
Garden catmint

LAMIACEAE

Nepeta is a summer-flowering herbaceous perennial that forms bushy mounds of soft, grey-green aromatic leaves when crushed, and produces spikes of small lavender-blue flowers throughout the summer months. The flowers are borne in whorls in profusion along the upright spikes.

It can be cut back during the summer if it becomes untidy, and will regrow and flower in a few weeks. Cutting back will actually encourage repeat flowering.

This is a plant loved by bees and butterflies for the nectar-rich flowers, but it is also adored by cats, who cannot get enough of its aromatic foliage, and will roll around in it, totally flattening it. A few short stakes or growing it through a support should resolve this.

The cultivar 'Six Hills Giant' is a taller plant to around 60 cm (24 in), with darker blue flowers.

ASPECT: Full sun.
FLOWERING: May – September.
HARDINESS: -10 to -15 °C (14 to 5 °F).

 30–45 cm (12–18 in)

30–45 cm (12–18 in)

OPHIOPOGON PLANISCAPUS 'NIGRESCENS'
Black mondo grass

ASPARAGACEAE

This grass-like evergreen perennial has leaves that are the darkest purple, which makes them look black, and they have a wonderful sheen to them. The sunnier their position the darker the leaves will be. The flat, leathery, strap-like leaves form small mounds that slowly spread by underground stems. During the summer they push up small flower spikes on which are borne purplish, bell-shaped flowers. The flowers are followed by shiny, black berries. As well as year-round and summer plantings, they can be used as an underplanting in mixed containers as part of a winter display, and look

Nepeta × faasenii 'Six Hills Giant'

Stachys byzantina 'Silver Carpet'

STACHYS BYZANTINA
Lamb's ears

LAMIACEAE

This is a plant long used for its superb foliage, which has certainly passed the test of time, and its common name 'lamb's ears' is very apt. The oval-shaped leaves are particularly soft and covered on both sides with whitish-grey, felty hairs.

It is an evergreen plant that is low-growing, spreading to make good ground cover, producing the same whitish-grey, soft hairs along its stems and flower spike, which has whorls of tiny pink flowers, slightly hidden by the hairs.

If you just want foliage, there is a non-flowering (rarely flowering) cultivar, *Stachys byzantina* 'Silver Carpet', that has all of the characteristic of the species above and is said to be the best silver form, and lower-growing, to around 15 cm (6 in) high.

Both are ideal as year-round ground cover between plants, or at the front of a sunny border. Occasionally they lose their leaves in cold wet winters, but they are replaced with fresh ones in spring.

ASPECT: Full sun or partial shade.
FLOWERING: July – September.
HARDINESS: -15 to -20 °C (5 to -4 °F).

 10–30 cm (4–12 in)

50 cm–1 m (20 in–3 ft)

Verbena bonariensis

VERBENA BONARIENSIS
Argentinian vervain

VERBENACEAE

A perfect plant for giving you graceful height in a border planting, this ornamental perennial has tall, branching, slender stems, with very few leaves, which are oblong with lobed margins. The tall stems are topped with tight clusters of lavender or lilac-purple flowers that are a magnet for bees and butterflies, which enjoy the long flowering season. At the end of the year the whole plant dies back to below ground, regrowing the following spring.

A very popular plant for growing in a mixed herbaceous border, it can be a bit of a thug, freely self-seeding itself all over the garden. But the seedlings are easily removed if not wanted.

Because of the tall, almost bare stems, *Verbena bonariensis* looks great growing with and through grasses, which also give them some support.

ASPECT: Full sun.
FLOWERING: June – October.
HARDINESS: -5 to -10 °C (23 to 14 °F).

 1.5–2 m (5–7 ft)

10–50 cm (4–20 in)

Shrubs

ARGYROCYTISUS BATTANDIERI
Moroccan broom
FABACEAE

(Formerly known as *Cytisus battandieri*)
As its common name suggests, this large deciduous shrub is native to the Atlas Mountains of Morocco. It is semi-deciduous, so in warmer areas will keep its foliage all year. The large trifoliate, soft, silvery leaves give the whole plant a silver-grey appearance, and it is transformed during midsummer when the tall, lupin-like pea flowers are borne in dense plumes of bright yellow, fragrant flower spikes. These give off a very distinctive, strong pineapple scent. Another common name for this shrub is the pineapple broom. Like all scented plants it is best planted where it will be passed by or close to a garden or patio seating area where the scent can be enjoyed.

It will do particularly well if grown against a sunny south- or west-facing wall where it will benefit from this warmer, sheltered aspect.

Argyrocytisus battandieri 'Yellow Tail' – is a smaller cultivar, with a bushier habit, more suited to a smaller garden or smaller space.

Any pruning should be carried out in summer after flowering.

ASPECT: Full sun.
FLOWERING: June – July.
HARDINESS: -10 to -15 °C (14 to 5 °F).

2 – 5 m (7 – 16 ft)
3 – 5 m (10 – 16 ft)

BRACHYGLOTTIS (DUNEDIN GROUP)
'Sunshine'
ASTERACEAE

Both the young silvery-green leaves and stems of this attractive shrub are felted with soft white hairs, which is what

PREVIOUS PAGE
Drought tolerant *Brachyglottis* provides attractive flowers and foliage

Argyrocytisus battandieri

Brachyglottis 'Sunshine'

gives this plant its overall silvery look. As the new leaves mature, they do lose the felt-hairs and become darker green. The bright yellow daisy flowers are an excellent contrast to the silvery foliage. The mature plant forms a dense, wide mound.

This versatile plant can also be clipped as a hedge to a height of around 1 m (3 ft), but flowering will be interrupted. Often used in building and landscape designs, it is super tough and extremely drought-tolerant.

The Dunedin Group refers to the crosses and backcrosses made between different

species, not all known. *Brachyglottis* 'Sunshine' is thought to be a cross between *B. compacta* and *B. laxifolia*.

Regular pruning is necessary as *Brachyglottis* does not always respond well to being pruned too hard into the old wood. Any pruning that is done should be after flowering.

ASPECT: Full sun to partial shade.
FLOWERING: June – July.
HARDINESS: -5 to -10 °C (23 to 14 °F).

1 – 1.5 m (3 – 5 ft)
1 – 1.5 m (3 – 5 ft)

BUDDLEJA ALTERNIFOLIA
Alternate-leaved butterfly bush
SCROPHULARIACEAE

This variety is very different from most other buddlejas, and not commonly seen in gardens, but it is easily recognisable with its graceful, weeping habit making it a highly attractive shrub. The long, arching branches grow almost to the ground, and bear small, silvery-grey leaves. The branches are covered in clusters of lilac-purple, sweetly scented flowers, which as with all buddlejas attract many beneficial insects, particularly butterflies.

Flowering in midsummer, *Buddleja alternifolia* should have the old flowering shoots pruned back to new growth once the current season flowers are over. Also, this is a good time to remove some of the oldest wood congesting the shrub, cutting back to the ground. As it flowers on previous seasons' growth this will give the plant plenty of time to produce more flowering wood for the following year.

ASPECT: Full sun to partial shade.
FLOWERING: June –July.
HARDINESS: -15 to -20 °C (5 to -4 °F).

 3–4 m (10–13 ft)

3–4 m (10–13 ft)

BUDDLEJA DAVIDII
Butterfly bush
SCROPHULARIACEAE

This buddleja species must be one of the most drought-tolerant plants you can grow. The seedlings find themselves in some of the most obscure places, particularly cracks in pavements and in the walls of derelict buildings, where they will happily flourish with almost total disregard to the lack of water and scorching temperatures. They thrive on neglect, freely naturalising any ground left untended, flowering no matter what is thrown at them.

As their common name butterfly bush suggests, their rich supply of nectar attracts butterflies, but they are also a magnet for many other insects. Bees and hoverflies are just two that on sunny days will feed on the numerous flowers with their sweet nectar.

Buddleja davidii is a deciduous medium-sized shrub with long racemes containing numerous small individual trumpet-shaped flowers from mid to late summer. The flower colours are found in various shades of purple, with the cultivars displaying many more colour variations from white (*Buddleja davidii* 'Nanhoensis Alba') to almost black, like *Buddleja* 'Black Knight' (a very deep purple), with many other colours and shades in between.

Once a framework is established, which should form an open goblet or stag's horn shape with an open centre, prune in spring back to four or five buds. This will promote lots of new growth and flowers. Unlike *Buddleja alternifolia*, *B. davidii* flowers on current season's growth.

ASPECT: Full sun to partial shade.
FLOWERING: July – September.
HARDINESS: -15 to -20 °C (5 to -4 °F).

 2.5–4 m (8–13 ft)

4–6 m (13–20 ft)

BUDDLEJA GLOBOSA
Orange ball tree
SCROPHULARIACEAE

Very different from the common buddlejas, this large evergreen shrub (semi-deciduous in the coldest winters) is vigorous and will grow very large if left unpruned. It is a fantastic plant, which in summer produces sweetly scented balls of striking, bright orange flowers, made up from dozens of small, densely packed individuals. Each of these rounded balls of flowers sits on short stems in loose clusters, making them even more prominent, as if their colour alone wasn't enough. Buddlejas are well known for attracting butterflies from which they

Buddleja davidii 'Nanhoensis Alba'

Buddleja davidii

Bupleurum fruticosum

BUPLEURUM FRUTICOSUM
Shrubby hare's-ear
APIACEAE

Its glossy, leathery, blue-green, narrowly oval leaves make this a very attractive, rounded, evergreen shrub, which produces an abundance of sulphur-yellow umbels of flowers on long stems throughout the summer. The flowers are very attractive to pollinating insects, particularly hoverflies.

The first time I came across this plant was on the Rock of Gibraltar, a large limestone ridge on the south coast of Spain. Subsequently I've seen it in other southern Spanish regions, often growing close to the coast, so it is a shrub tolerant of maritime conditions. It thrives in Mediterranean locations, and a hot, sunny spot in a garden border or courtyard is an ideal position.

Although fairly slow-growing it can become a bit untidy or too large for its space after five years or so, but does respond well to pruning, which is best done in the spring. It can be cut right back to ground level, and will regrow the same season, but not produce flowers again until the following year.

ASPECT: Full sun to partial shade.
FLOWERING: June – September.
HARDINESS: -5 to -10 °C (23 to 14 °F).

 1.5–2 m (5–7 ft)

1.5–2 m (5–7 ft)

CARPENTERIA CALIFORNICA
Tree anemone
HYDRANGEACEAE

This is a fabulous summer-flowering, bushy, evergreen shrub that will do best if it has a sheltered spot. It makes quite an upright shrub that spreads a little with age. It has dark green, glossy leaves and peeling bark on the mature stems. But its crowning glory is the pure white, saucer-shaped, fragrant, anemone-like flowers,

get their common name, butterfly bush. Well, this buddleja should perhaps be called the 'bee bush' as at its flowering peak each ball is often almost completely covered with bees gorging on its sweet nectar.

It will also tolerate some shade, so would do well in an area of the garden that can be sometimes difficult to fill.

It should be pruned each year after flowering, taking out the oldest stem to the ground, and flowered growth back to a strong bud, to encourage good flowering wood for the following year.

ASPECT: Full sun to partial shade.
FLOWERING: June – August.
HARDINESS: -15 to -20 °C (5 to -4 °F).

 4–6 m (13–20 ft)

4–6 m (13–20 ft)

with showy yellow stamens. The flowers are borne in loose, terminal clusters. Altogether a very ornamental and prolific flowering plant.

The cultivar *Carpenteria californica* 'Bodnant' is said to be hardier, have larger flowers and a longer flowering season. Each year remove a few of the oldest branches after flowering, and any frost-damaged tips in the spring.

ASPECT: Full sun.

FLOWERING: June – July.

HARDINESS: -5 to -10 °C (23 to 14 °F).

 1–2.5 m (3–8 ft)

1–2.5 m (3–8 ft)

CERATOSTIGMA WILLMOTTIANUM
Chinese plumbago

PLUMBAGINACEAE

This deciduous shrub is native to China and really comes to life in the autumn, when it is at its best. During the spring and early summer new shoots appear through the remnants of the previous year's growth. Although it is classed as a shrub it dies back most years, more like an herbaceous perennial! But then in some years the framework will persist.

The gentian-blue flowers are a delight, and they somehow intensify in colour in fading evening light. The bristly green foliage is transformed in the autumn, turning fiery shades of reds, and contrasts wonderfully with the pale-centred blue flowers.

Ceratostigma plumbaginoides – is an herbaceous perennial with similar blue flowers, dying back in the winter. It has a creeping habit, spreading by underground runners, only growing to around 30 cm (12 in) tall, with good autumn leaf colour. It makes a good choice for late-season colour at the front of a border.

Any pruning should be carried out just as the new growth starts to appear,

The late flowers of this small shrub are produced among its bright red autumn leaves

Ceratostigma willmottianum

removing dead stems and the rest back close to ground level as *Ceratostigma* produces flowers on the current season's growth.

ASPECT: Full sun to partial shade.

FLOWERING: August – October.

HARDINESS: -5 to -10 °C (23 to 14 °F).

 50 cm–1 m (20 in–3 ft)

1–1.5 m (3–5 ft)

CONVOLVULUS CNEORUM
Shrubby bindweed

CONVOLVULACEAE

This is a dwarf, low-spreading evergreen shrub, with soft silvery foliage. It has to have good drainage, and if it can be elevated and planted at the top of a bank, or sprawling over a wall, where drainage will be improved, so much the better. It

requires a hot sunny spot to thrive.

In early spring attractive pink buds are formed, which open into pale pink and white, funnel-shaped flowers with a yellow centre. Each petal has a pink, flushed vein in the centre. *Convolvulus cneorum* also makes a good plant for growing in a container.

These are fairly low-maintenance plants that require little or no pruning, and any pruning to tidy plants should be done immediately after flowering.

ASPECT: Full sun.

FLOWERING: May – July.

HARDINESS: -5 to -10 °C (23 to 14 °F).

 30–50 cm (12–20 in)

50–75 cm (20–30 in)

CISTUS
Rock roses
CISTACEAE

I think if I could only pick one genus of plants to have in a garden for drought-tolerant and sun-loving plants then it would be *Cistus*. The species come in all shapes, sizes and colours, from *Cistus ladanifer*, which can grow more than 3 m (10 ft) tall, to ground-hugging plants like *Cistus crispus* or the prostrate form of *Cistus salviifolius*. And then there are a multitude of cultivars, almost too many to choose from.

The crumpled petals make these pretty shrubs look fragile, but they are nothing of the sort. In their native habitats they thrive in poor, impoverished soils, enduring months of dry, baking heat, producing a new flush of flowers every day, which fall during the hottest part of the day only to be replaced the following day. In less

Bees just love cistus flowers, the centres of which are filled with a mass of pollen producing stamens

Cistus albidus

harsh British conditions, the flowers last longer into the afternoon. Most *Cistus* will tolerate most soil types, although *Cistus ladanifer* is only found growing in acidic soils, but it will still grow in alkaline soils that are close to neutral. We have plants of *C. ladanifer* growing at Kew that are more than 30 years old in a pH of around 7.5.

They all require a free-draining soil that doesn't hold water, as cold, wet soil in winter will rot their roots.

Below are just a selection of the species and cultivars. All are evergreen.

CISTUS ALBIDUS – has soft, felty, grey, unstalked leaves that are covered on both surfaces with fine hairs. The leaves contrast beautifully with the clusters of lilac to rose-pink flowers, which have delicate, crumpled petals, tinged yellow at their base below the numerous orange stamens. There is also a natural white form, *Cistus albidus* f. *albus*. Height 1 m (3 ft) × spread 75 cm (30 in).

CISTUS CRISPUS – a small *Cistus*, forming small mounds. Its leaves are coarsely hairy and have a wavy margin. They are deep pink and only around 5 cm (2 in) across. In the wild this little

Cistus in Kew's Mediterranean Garden

shrub often hybridises with *Cistus albidus*, producing an intermediate that yields fertile seeds. Height 15 cm (6 in) × spread 60 cm (24 in).

CISTUS LADANIFER – is the tallest of all the species and prefers acid soils, but will still do well in neutral soil. Not only is it the tallest, but it also has the largest flowers, which are solitary and around 10 cm (4 in) across. The leaves of this species become sticky and aromatic in the summer heat, and it is from their young leaves and stems that the sticky gum, ladanum, exudes. This sticky gum has long been collected for incense and perfumes. Height 3 m (10 ft) × spread 1 m (3 ft).

CISTUS LAURIFOLIUS – similar to *C. ladanifer* but grows in limestone areas and is the hardiest *Cistus*, naturally growing high in the mountains. It has single white flowers with a yellow centre, and the leaves are dark, glaucous-green, with wavy margins. The mature bark is a wonderful cinnamon-brown colour. Height 2 m (7 ft) × spread 2 m (7 ft).

CISTUS MONSPELIENSIS – is very floriferous, decorating the small, aromatic, deeply veined leaves with clusters of up to eight small white flowers, which are individually around 3 cm (1 in) across. Height 1 m (3 ft) × spread 1 m (3 ft).

CISTUS POPULIFOLIUS – is easily recognisable by its poplar-like leaves (heart-shaped), with wavy margins. The white flowers have a yellow centre and are held in small clusters of up to six individual flowers on a single hairy stalk. The flower buds are also very distinctive, with their red sepals.

This is another very hardy species. In the wild it is usually found above 600 m (around 2,000 ft). Height 1.5 m (5 ft) × spread 1.5 m (5 ft).

CISTUS SALVIIFOLIUS – has lovely white cup-shaped flowers with a yellow base, and as its species name *salviifolius* suggests, it has sage-like, textured leaves. It is an extremely variable plant that can be prostrate, scrambling over the ground, rocks and even through other plants. It can also make a dense, upright shrub over 1 m (3 ft) tall. Unlike most other *Cistus* it will tolerate some shade, making it versatile when it comes to placing it in the garden.

CISTUS × AGUILARI – tall and upright, with bright-green leaves that have wavy margins. The flowers are large and white, similar to *C. ladanifer*, one of the parents (along with *C. populifolius*). The cultivar 'Maculatus' has deep red blotches at the base of each petal and is the result of being backcrossed with *Cistus ladanifer*. Height 2.5 m (8 ft) × spread 1 m (3 ft).

CISTUS × CYPRIUS – is a hybrid that shows both of the best attributes of its parents, *C. ladanifer × C. laurifolius*, being tall and upright with dark green, glaucous leaves that shine with sticky resin in hot weather. It has large flowers, like both parents, around 8 cm (3 in) across, but with the blotching to the base of each petal that comes from *C. ladanifer*, which is red above a yellow base. Height 2 m (7 ft) × spread 3 m (10 ft).

CISTUS × FLORENTINUS – is a compact, little hybrid that shows more of the characteristics of the parent, *Cistus monspeliensis*, with the long leaves and more open, small white flowers. It does tolerate some shade for which its other parent, *Cistus salviifolius*, is known. Height 1.5 m (5 ft) × spread 1.5 m (5 ft).

CISTUS 'Grayswood Pink' – makes a low-spreading shrub with soft, silvery-green leaves, producing a profusion of lovely pale pink flowers, fading to white. This is my personal favourite hybrid and always has a place in any garden I own. It also does really well as a container plant, or ground cover in a gravel garden. Height 50 cm (20 in) × spread 3 m (10 ft).

CISTUS 'Jessamy Beauty' – is another cultivar that shows that it has *Cistus ladanifer* somewhere in its parentage, with its dark red, blotched petals. The large white, red, blotched flowers are around 6–7 cm (2–3 in) across, and the textured leaves are long and linear. Height 75 cm (30 in) × spread 2 m (7 ft).

CISTUS × PURPUREUS – is a standout plant in any garden, with its large (8 cm (3 in) across) purplish-pink overlapping petals, blotched deep red, and centred with a ball of yellow-orange stamens, set among long, narrow leaves. Its parents are *C. ladanifer × C. creticus*. Height 1.5 m (5 ft) × spread 1.5 m (5 ft).

Cistus will not tolerate any hard pruning into its old wood, so should be pruned after flowering during the summer, back to healthy buds. Sparse watering, and no feeding, is the best way to restrict the growth, and then little or no pruning is necessary.

ASPECT: Full sun.

FLOWERING: April – July.

HARDINESS: -5 to -10 °C (23 to 14 °F).

 Indicated individually

Indicated individually

CORONILLA VALENTINA SUBSP. GLAUCA
Glaucous scorpion-vetch
FABACEAE

A small, evergreen member of the pea family, this is a bushy shrub, with blue-green, glaucous pinnate leaves, which have obovate leaflets with notched tips (i.e. egg-shaped, with the narrower end at the base rather than the tip). The yellow pea-like flowers are borne in umbels of up to 15 fragrant individuals. It has a main flowering period in spring and early summer, but will continue to flower right through the year, including during the winter.

Coronilla have distinctive jointed seed pods, with a hooked tip, looking very much like a scorpion's tail, hence the common name scorpion-vetch. This is a shrub that freely seeds around, so will need to be regularly weeded out from areas where it is not wanted. Seedlings can be potted up, though, for use elsewhere in the garden or for gifts.

The cultivar 'Citrina' has paler, lemon-coloured flowers.

Any pruning required should be carried out in winter.

ASPECT: Full sun.
FLOWERING: April – May.
But will flower all year.
HARDINESS: -5 to -10 °C (23 to 14 °F).

 1–2 m (3–7 ft)

50 cm–1.5 m (20 in–5 ft)

Coronilla valentina 'Citrina'

DAPHNE LAUREOLA
Spurge laurel
THYMELAEACEAE

I think this is a very underused plant, with lots going for it. *Daphne laureola* will grow in the dry, shadier parts of a garden as well in full sun. Its winter flowering also extends the seasons of interest.

This evergreen shrub has an upright form, with thick, shiny, dark green leaves, which tend to grow in terminal clusters. Among the leaf axils are borne greenish-yellow, honey-scented flowers. It would really stand out during the winter growing through the purple winter leaves of a *Bergenia* such as the cultivar 'Beethoven', and being evergreen still has a place all year.

Daphne laureola subsp. *philippi* – is more compact, semi-prostrate and has a rounded habit, growing to around 50 cm (20 in) tall.

Minimal pruning is all that is needed, just to remove dead, or crossing branches, and should be carried out in early spring, after flowering.

ASPECT: Full sun to full shade.
FLOWERING: February – March.
HARDINESS: -10 to -15 °C (14 to 5 °F).

 75 cm–1 m (30 in–3 ft)

1–1.5 m (3–5 ft)

Daphne laureola* subsp. *philppi

ERIOBOTRYA JAPONICA
Loquat
ROSACEAE

A large shrub or small tree, native to China and Japan, loquat has impressive large, stiff, glossy, dark green lance-shaped leaves that are deeply veined, and up to 30 cm (12 in) long, giving it an exotic look. It flowers late in the season and sometimes into the new year, depending on weather. The fragrant white flowers are borne in large clusters. Unfortunately, they rarely produce the tasty orange, plum-shaped fruits, often seen when it is grown in Mediterranean gardens, and also commercially, owing to the flowers being damaged by frost, or not being pollinated during cold weather.

An ideal spot for it would be in a courtyard garden, or at the back of a large walled border in full sun, and maybe you will achieve some fruits in spring and early summer.

Because flowering is late in the year, producing fruit the following year in late spring, if you have to prune then late winter or early spring is best. But ideally loquats should be given the space to fully mature and will need very little pruning, except for tidying and removing any dead wood.

ASPECT: Full sun.
FLOWERING: October – December.
HARDINESS: -5 to -10 °C (23 to 14 °F).

4–8 m (13–26 ft)

4–8 m (13–26 ft)

EURYOPS TYSONII
Tyson's euruops
ASTERACEAE

A late-flowering, multi-branched, bushy evergreen with an upright habit, native to South Africa, which makes a very attractive small garden shrub. Its stems are densely covered in small leathery

Eriobotrya japonica

leaves. The sweet-scented, yellow, daisy-like flowers are around 10 mm (0.4 in) in diameter and produced profusely for a long period throughout the summer months at the tips of the stems.

Very little pruning is necessary, other than cutting back lightly after flowering, and to keep plant in bounds.

ASPECT: Full sun.
FLOWERING: June – October.
HARDINESS: 0 to -5 °C (32 to 23 °F).

50 cm–1 m (20 in–3 ft)

50 cm–1 m (20 in–3 ft)

Euryops tysonii

MELIANTHUS MAJOR
Honey flower
MELIANTHEACEAE

Melianthus major is similar to *Melianthus comosus* in many ways, though the evergreen, grey-green, pinnate leaves are larger, and the overall size of the plant is also taller.

It needs a good summer to flower in the UK. The crimson, sweetly scented flowers emerge on long, drooping spikes. They will produce plenty of leaf wet or dry, but the best chance of getting them to flower is if they are kept on the dry side. Our best flowering plants at Kew are grown in a gravel garden.

Similarly, as with *M. comosus*, it will put up with some frost, but a hard frost will damage the foliage. In these circumstances cut the whole plant back to ground level and mulch. The following spring you should get new regrowth. This can also be used as a method each year to restrict the size.

Both species can also be grown in a large container and brought into a cool greenhouse or conservatory in the winter.

Melianthus major 'Purple Haze' – is a cultivar with deep purple tones and a more compact habit.

ASPECT: Full sun.

FLOWERING: April – June.

HARDINESS: 0 to -5 °C (32 to 23 °F).

 1.5–2.5 m (5–8 ft)

1.5–2.5 m (5–8 ft)

MYRTUS COMMUNIS
Common myrtle
MYRTACEAE

An aromatic, evergreen, upright shrub, with small, oval, glossy, dark green leaves, that have a pointed tip. The leaves are fragrant when crushed. The dark year-round foliage is a good backdrop to paler colours, particularly in the winter. During early summer the pink buds borne on individual stems open into wonderfully showy, pure white, sweet-scented, solitary flowers, covering the whole plant. When fully open the petals become slightly reflexed to accommodate the mass of white stamens, topped with creamy-yellow anthers, followed by bluish-black berries when fully ripe.

This is definitely in my top ten shrubs for a drought-tolerant garden. Whether in a gravel bed, border, courtyard, patio or container it will not disappoint. It may need some winter protection in colder areas.

The leaves and fruits of myrtle are used as flavourings and in perfumes. In Corsica and Sardinia the berries are steeped in alcohol, much the same as we use sloes (blackthorn fruits) to produce liquors.

ASPECT: Full sun.

FLOWERING: June – August.

HARDINESS: 0 to -5 °C (32 to 23 °F).

 2–3 m (7–10 ft)

1–1.5 m (3–5 ft)

Myrtus communis

NANDINA DOMESTICA
Heavenly bamboo
BERBERIDACEAE

An erect, medium-sized, upright evergreen shrub (occasionally semi-evergreen in colder areas), with stiff, upright, small cane-like stems that are said to be bamboo-like.

The younger branches and foliage are in contrast much lighter, which is primarily what *Nandina* is grown for, the small pointed oval-shaped leaves starting out light green, tinged pinkish-red, and developing richer reds as the season progresses.

During the summer it produces panicles of small, star-shaped, white flowers that are followed by bright red berries after a hot summer. Nandinas are fairly slow-growing and spread by underground runners, which can be removed once the clump has reached the desired size or used to replant elsewhere.

The cultivar 'Fire Power' is slightly more compact and has a stronger autumn colour of fiery oranges and reds. It is a good plant for a container, where its showy year-round appeal can be appreciated. You will need more than one plant if you want berries, as there are separate male and female plants. 'Richmond' is a hermaphrodite cultivar that will produce berries if you only have room for a single plant.

ASPECT: Full sun.

FLOWERING: July – August.

HARDINESS: -10 to -15 °C (14 to 5 °F).

 1–1.5 m (3–5 ft)

1–1.5 m (3–5 ft)

NERIUM OLEANDER
Oleander
APOCYNACEAE

Oleander has a very varied habitat. The first time I came across this plant it was growing along streams, river courses and

Nerium oleander

OLEARIA MACRODONTA
Daisy bush
ASTERACEAE

A medium-sized evergreen shrub originating from New Zealand, daisy bush has peeling, tan-coloured bark and glossy, greyish-green, holly-like leaves. These are softer than actual holly leaves, with spiny margins but with soft white hairs on their underside. The daisy-like, fragrant flowers are produced in profusion, and are borne in large clusters. Individual flowers have white, rounded petals and a reddish-brown eye in their centre. These are very attractive to bees and butterflies.

This plant is both drought- and salt-tolerant, making it an ideal shrub for coastal areas.

It is a plant with foliage that looks good all year round, can be used as an alternative for hedging and will take hard pruning. *Olearia macrodonta* should be pruned in the spring (April) each year to keep it neat and tidy.

ASPECT: Full sun.
FLOWERING: June – July.
HARDINESS: -5 to -10 °C (23 to 14 °F).

 2–4 m (7–13 ft)

2–4 m (7–13 ft)

ORIGANUM DICTAMNUS
Cretan dittany
LAMIACEAE

The aromatic leaves of *Origanum* have been used both dried and fresh as a culinary herb for centuries. There always seems to be some confusion over oregano and marjoram. Both oregano and marjoram are types (in the same genus) of *Origanum* but are different species. Marjoram is from *Origanum majorana* and is milder and sweeter than oregano (*Origanum vulgare*).

Origanum dictamnus is an aromatic plant that is endemic to the Greek island of Crete. I particularly like it because

areas that were often flooded. I presumed that it was a plant that would only grow happily in damp soils. Then I was later to find out it also flourishes in the desert areas of Morocco! An extremely versatile plant indeed. I should have guessed when I saw oleander planted along the central reservations on the motorways in southern Spain. Any plant that can stand the blistering summer Andalusian heat and vehicle pollution has to be tough. So a drought-tolerant garden situation is a pushover. It is a bit frost-tender and will need protection in cold areas; frost pockets must be avoided.

Oleander is a multi-stemmed evergreen shrub, or small tree. As a shrub it makes a large open mound. The dark green leaves are long and lance-shaped, with a prominent paler midrib. The most common colour for the flowers Is pinkish-red, but colour varies in the wild, with dark red as well as white occasionally found. There are many cultivars available that include all of these colours, including double-flowered and variegated forms. The five-petalled flowers are borne in terminal clusters of individual flowers, around 4–5 cm (1.5–2 in) across, and a frilly striped hairy throat. The distinctive paired seed heads are long, woody and of pencil thickness; they split open to reveal small seeds attached to a fluffy structure, which helps them float away on the wind.

Care should be taken as all parts of this plant are poisonous if ingested. The leaves have a superficial resemblance to *Olea europaea*, the olive, or to *Laurus nobilis*, sweet bay, which are used as a flavouring. Oleander leaves are much fleshier, and when you remove them, they exude a milky-white sap.

ASPECT: Full sun.
FLOWERING: July – October.
HARDINESS: 0 to -5 °C (32 to 23 °F).

 2–3 m (7–10 ft)

1.5–2.5 m (5–8 ft)

SANTOLINA CHAMAECYPARISSUS
Cotton lavender

ASTERACEAE

This highly aromatic little evergreen
shrub is very drought-tolerant. I've seen
it growing in limestone rock crevices in
mountains that are totally dry in summer,
apart from some occasional moisture
from low clouds, and then covered with
snow in winter. A very tough little plant
indeed.

It forms small, rounded mounds
of silver-grey linear foliage, which is
covered in fine hairs, and has deeply
lobed margins. When not in flower they
are like small, silver cushions, but are
transformed when in flower, with each
flowerhead on a separate stem, and the
whole plant covered by a mass of small,
deep yellow, button-like flowerheads
around 1–1.5 cm (0.4–0.6 in) wide.

Overwatering should be avoided, as it
results in lush leggy plants that are prone
to disease.

ASPECT: Full sun.

FLOWERING: June – August.

HARDINESS: -10 to -15 °C (14 to 5 °F).

 10–50 cm (4–20 in)

50–75 cm (20–30 in)

Santolina chamaecyparissus

Tanacetum densum **subsp.** *amani*

SENECIO CINERARIA
Silver ragwort

ASTERACEAE

An evergreen sub-shrub with handsome
silver-grey foliage, soft and felty to the
touch, it can be slightly tender, but more
to cold wet than frost. For that reason it
is often grown as an annual. It is a plant
mainly prized for its foliage, which is
very attractive deeply cut, and silver. I
personally quite like the yellow daisy-like
flowers that bloom in midsummer, but
these are often removed to encourage
more leafy growth. The cultivar 'Silver
Dust' has even more deeply cut leaves.

ASPECT: Full sun.

FLOWERING: June – July.

HARDINESS: 0 to -5 °C (32 to 23 °F).

 40–60 cm (16–24 in)

30–50 cm (12–20 in)

TANACETUM DENSUM
SUBSP. *AMANI*
Partridge feather

ASTERACEAE

This low-growing evergreen foliage plant
forms mounds of the most amazing soft,
feathery, silver-grey, finely cut, almost
fern-like leaves. It is mainly grown for its
foliage, but it does produce small yellow,
button-like flowers in terminal branched
clusters. Suited to a gravel garden where
the silver-grey leaves will look their best.
Also makes a good container plant.

Being fairly slow-spreading, no pruning
is really necessary, apart from restricting
spread, as the new leaves cover up the
older ones as they fade.

ASPECT: Full sun.

FLOWERING: June – July.

HARDINESS: 0 to -5 °C (32 to 23 °F).

 10–20 cm (4–8 in)

30–50 cm (12–20 in)

TEUCRIUM CHAMAEDRYS
Wall germander
LAMIACEAE

This small evergreen sub-shrub is an absolute magnet for bees. The whole plant is aromatic, and somewhat hairy, producing long spikes of pinkish or mauve flowers over a long period throughout the summer. Wall germander spreads by creeping underground stems, but relatively slowly.

This tough little plant is often seen self-seeded growing out of walls and has naturalised itself in parts of Britain.

There is also a white-flowered form, *Teucrium chamaedrys* f. *albiflora*.

It can be grown as a low border-edging plant, making an attractive low hedge. Trimmed over in spring, it will keep neat and compact.

ASPECT: Full sun to partial shade.
FLOWERING: July – September.
HARDINESS: -10 to -15 °C (14 to 5 °F).

 10–30 cm (4–12 in)

20–40 cm (8–16 in)

Shrubby germander makes a great evergreen, flowering, small hedge

Teucrium fruticans

Teucrium chamaedrys

TEUCRIUM FRUTICANS
Shrubby germander
LAMIACEAE

A small evergreen shrub, with a greyish-green overall appearance resulting from the stems (which are four-cornered) and undersides of its aromatic leaves being covered in fine white hairs. They are a glossy, dark green above.

It forms a bushy plant of tangled branches, which makes it quite dense, and if clipped will actually make a pretty flowering small hedge. The pale blue-lilac flowers are quite unusual and stand out well against the darker foliage. The flowers are produced in terminal clusters, and normally open in pairs. They have no top lip, but prominent arching stamens above a large lower lip that has five lobes patterned with darker markings, with the lower lobe being the largest. This flower arrangement is characteristic of this genus of plants.

ASPECT: Full sun.
FLOWERING: June – August.
HARDINESS: 0 to -5 °C (32 to 23 °F).

 1–2 m (3–7 ft)

1–2 m (3–7 ft)

TEUCRIUM POLIUM
Felty germander
LAMIACEAE

A small, much-branched evergreen shrubby plant from the Mediterranean, which like many plants from this region has adaptations making it suited to hot, dry conditions, with in-rolled leaf margins reducing the leaf surface and a dense covering of fine hairs to trap moisture.

The dense covering of hairs gives this low-growing *Teucrium* a silvery-white appearance, which goes well at the front of a gravel bed in full sun. During summer small domed heads are formed, with many tiny individual white flowers.

Very little maintenance is needed apart from removing the odd bit of die-back.

ASPECT: Full sun.
FLOWERING: June – August.
HARDINESS: 0 to -5 °C (32 to 23 °F).

 10–30 cm (4–12 in)

1–2 m (3–7 ft)

Succulents

AEONIUM ARBOREUM
Tree houseleek

CRASSULACEAE

Although not fully hardy this is such a good architectural plant that it needs a mention. It's a must for any drought-tolerant summer scheme. This plant gives a tropical feel to a garden and is really set off when grown in a dry gravel garden, in and around rocks. But it looks and does equally well as a dot plant in a bed or border, treated as summer bedding.

Aeoniums are evergreen succulent plants with arching stems bearing terminal rosettes of fleshy leaves that are almost spoon-shaped. It is from the centre of these leaf rosettes on mature plants that the flower stems emerge, producing clusters of small, bright yellow, star-like flowers in late spring. Unfortunately, the flowering stem often dies after flowering.

PREVIOUS PAGE
Yucca rostrata makes a dramatic talking point in the garden

Aeoniums make great conservatory container plants, where they are most likely to flower, and can be put out for the summer on a patio or plunged in a bed or border and then brought back in for the winter and not watered through their dormant season. The dark-leaved forms may lighten or even begin to green up, but this is to do with light levels, and they will darken again during late spring and summer.

Aeonium arboreum is jade-green in colour, but more popular are the dark-leaved forms, *Aeonium* 'Atropupureum' (deep red-purple) and 'Zwartkop' (very dark purple, almost black). For a mix of the two try *Aeonium* 'Blushing Beauty', which has rosettes of green leaves tinged with red. There is also a green and white variety, *Aeonium arboreum* 'Variegatum', which has cream flowers in spring.

Aeoniums rarely if ever need any form of pruning. Cutting them down when they get too tall and spindly can improve their overall appearance, getting them to form several new heads.

Aeonium arboreum

ASPECT: Full sun.
FLOWERING: March – May.
HARDINESS: Not hardy.

 1–1.5 m (3–5 ft)

1 m (3 ft)

The spikey habit of agaves can give a dramatic contrast to other plants, particularly when planted in gravel

Agave montana

ACACIA DEALBATA
Silver wattle
FABACEAE

The wattles or mimosa are a very large group of plants of tropical and subtropical parts of the world, with by far the largest number of different species coming from Australia (approximately 1,000 species).

Acacia dealbata is best grown in a sunny, sheltered spot, for example against a south- or west-facing wall as it does need a little protection from cold winds, but is hardy down to -5 °C (23 °F). If badly frost-damaged, it will generally regrow from the base. It is a particularly good trained as a wall shrub.

It is a large evergreen shrub or small tree, and in ideal conditions can grow up to 8 m (26 ft) tall. It has grey-green, feathery foliage and attractive fluffy pompoms of bright yellow, fragrant flowers in spring. The common name wattle comes from its use for wattle and daub in buildings by early settlers in Australia, as the wood is very pliable.

It does not like hard pruning, and

Acacia dealbata

PREVIOUS PAGE Stone pines – *Pinus pinea*

Acca sellowiana

pruning should be done after flowering in late spring, whether to train a good framework for a wall shrub or just to restrict its size.

ASPECT: Full sun, to full shade.
FLOWERING: February – April.
HARDINESS: 1 to -5 °C (34 to 23 °F).

 5–10 m (16–33 ft)

3–4 m (10–13 ft)

ACCA SELLOWIANA
Pineapple guava
MYRTACEAE

A slow-growing evergreen tree or large shrub, native to South America, which prefers light shade in a south-west-facing spot, but which will tolerate full sun. It is fairly hardy. There are two specimens in Kew Gardens (one of which is over 5 m (16 ft) tall and 50 years old), growing with the protection of a 3 m (10 ft) wall, that have seen temperatures down as low as -12 °C (10 °F).

Acca sellowiana produce multi-stemmed plants with leaves that are glossy-green above and densely covered in white felted hairs beneath. The flowers are very tropical-looking, with white

Acca fruit

petals, flushed crimson inside, that reflex when fully open to reveal numerous bright crimson stamens, topped with creamy anthers. These flowers are edible.

This exotic-looking plant also has the added bonus once mature of producing edible fruits in the autumn, after seasons with long hot summers. The fruits are long, with green rippled skin, and egg-shaped. The flavour is quite complex, definitely featuring pineapple as in its common name, but it mostly reminds me of bubble-gum! All the people I have asked to try them have tasted something different, but they all agreed they were delicious.

Generally, evergreens are pruned just before growth stars in mid-spring, but because this is when *Acca* starts flowering it is best left until after it finishes. They need very little pruning, though, apart from removing dead or diseased wood.

ASPECT: Full sun.
FLOWERING: May – August.
HARDINESS: 0 to -12 °C (32 to 10 °F).

 5 m (16 ft)

3 m (10 ft)

ACER MONSPESSULANUM
Montpellier maple
SAPINDACEAE

A great tree for a small garden, the common name comes from this plant's discovery in the south of France, referring to the French city of Montpellier.

In favourable conditions this slow-growing tree can reach a height of 8–10 m (26–33 ft), but is more likely to mature at around 3–5 m (10–16 ft) tall. *Acer monspessulanum* differs from many other acers in having a leaf with three distinct lobes that are evenly sized, individually held on long stalks. The upper leaf surface is glossy green, and it is lighter on the underside. Flowers are produced in spring on long pendant racemes, and are yellow-green in colour.

The winged seeds (samaras) are bright red, contrasting with the glossy green foliage, which during autumn turns a mix of yellow and orange tones.

Acers should not be pruned in early spring, as the pruning cuts bleed quite badly. Pruning should be carried out in late summer or early autumn.
ASPECT: Full sun to partial shade.
FLOWERING: April – May.
HARDINESS: -15 to -20 °C (5 to -4 °F).

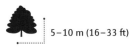

5–10 m (16–33 ft)

4–5 m (13–16 ft)

ALBIZIA JULIBRISSIN
Silk tree
FABACEAE

Albizia is a small tree that would be equally at home in a small courtyard garden, a dry gravel garden or garden border. It is deciduous and grows to a height of between 3 and 8 m (10 and 26 ft) tall, usually on the smaller side when grown outside of its native habitat range of China and Iran.

It has exotic, showy-looking flowers that sit up above the attractive feather-

A medium sized tree, great for a small garden. Glossy green leaves in summer, turning autumnal yellow and orange at the end of the year.

Acer monspessulanum

like foliage, which is made up of tiny crescent-shaped leaflets, angled bipinnately along long stalks of drooping branches. The flowers themselves are produced in dense clusters of fluffy pale-pink individuals. Their long purple-red stamens make them really stand out. If you want a small tree that will be a talking point, then this is the one.

There are also varieties with dark-coloured foliage, including 'Chocolate Fountain' and 'Summer Chocolate'.

Pruning needed to restrict growth should be done during the spring, pruning back the previous year's growth.
ASPECT: Full sun.
FLOWERING: June – August.
HARDINESS: -5 to -10 °C (23 to 14 °F).

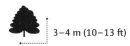

3–4 m (10–13 ft)

2–3 m (7–10 ft)

Albizia julibrissin

ARBUTUS UNEDO
Strawberry tree
ERICACEAE

A beautiful, ornamental, small, evergreen tree that can either be grown on a single stem as a specimen or as a multi-stemmed shrub. *Arbutus* is in the same family as heathers and so prefers an acid soil, but will still grow in a neutral soil and will even tolerate alkaline soils.

It has glossy, dark green leaves and produces panicles of the typical bell-shaped flowers of the heather family. The flowers are white, appearing in the autumn, and usually grow alongside the attractive-looking red mature fruits, which are the product of the previous year's flowers. The two hanging together add to the tree's ornamental value.

The fruits are edible, gritty and a bit bland, and are definitely an acquired taste. The Roman naturalist Pliny the Elder is supposed to have commented 'I only eat one', from which the Latin *unedo* is derived, referring to their unusual taste. Personally, I quite like them. They have to be fully ripe, though.

Arbutus unedo 'Rubra' – this plant differs from the straight species in having dark pink flowers, rather than white. It was originally discovered growing wild in Ireland in the 1800s.

Prune once new growth starts to appear in spring, and after the risk of late frost has passed. Very little pruning is usually needed apart from removing dead or damaged branches.

ASPECT: Full sun.
FLOWERING: October – December.
HARDINESS: -10 to -15 °C (14 to 5 °F).

4–8 m (13–26 ft)

4–6 m (13–20 ft)

OPPOSITE *Quercus suber* (see page 138)

Arbutus unedo

CELTIS AUSTRALIS
Nettle tree
CANNABACEAE

This medium-sized deciduous tree has beautifully shiny, smooth grey bark, which peels with age. The overall shape is a rounded, open crown.

It gets its common name from the long, pointed nettle-like leaves, which have sharply toothed margins and are rough on both surfaces, often looking a bit chlorotic in the summer. The small, inconspicuous greenish flowers produced in spring attract bees and butterflies. Small, round, red-brown or black fruits ripen in the late autumn, and are edible, although the seed is quite large in comparison to the fruit, so there is very little of the sweet, edible flesh.

The autumn colour is variable. In a good year it turns yellow.

If needed, any pruning should be carried out during late winter and early spring while the plant is dormant. Any branches that need to be removed should be cut out while they are relatively small, as large cuts are slow to heal.

ASPECT: Full sun.
FLOWERING: March – April.
HARDINESS: -10 to -15 °C (14 to 5 °F).

10–15 m (33–49 ft)

5–8 m (16–26 ft)

Cercis siliquastrum

CERCIS SILIQUASTRUM
Judas tree
FABACEAE

For me this is one of the delights of a garden in spring. It is a bushy deciduous shrub that is absolutely transformed when its leafless branches are clothed in thousands of cerise-purple flowers almost covering the entire tree (sometimes including the trunk). The better the previous summer the better the flowering will be the following spring. As the flowers fade, new heart-shaped leaves appear, bronze-coloured at first, turning an attractive bright green. In autumn the yellow leaves contrast with the clusters of long, reddish-purple seed pods.

In the Mediterranean Garden within Kew Gardens is a wonderful old multi-stemmed specimen, which now sprawls on the ground, as if resting its weary limbs, but continues to give a magnificent display of its flower power every year.

Prune during the dormant period, between late autumn and spring. But any dead branches should be removed in early summer, when they can be more easily spotted. They can also be pruned

very hard if rejuvenation is needed, and again this should be done while dormant.
ASPECT: Full sun to partial shade.
FLOWERING: April – May.
HARDINESS: -10 to -15 °C (14 to 5 °F).

3–6 m (10–20 ft)

4–10 m (13–33 ft)

CUPRESSUS SEMPERVIRENS
Pencil cypress
CUPRESSACEAE

The form of *Cupressus sempervirens* that is mostly grown as an ornamental tree is sometimes known as the *stricta* form, and is a tall and narrow conifer, giving it the common name of the pencil cypress. Another of its common names is the Italian cypress, although it's not native to Italy. This tall, narrow form is not known in the wild. *C. sempervirens* is an evergreen conifer native to the eastern Mediterranean region where it can make a large spreading tree.

Throughout the Mediterranean the narrow form is a statuesque tree that is an impressive sight in many hill villages and towns, particularly in Italy.

There are many cultivars, some of the more common ones including 'Pyramidalis', 'Totem Pole' and 'Green Pencil'.

Some summer pruning may be needed to keep the tall, narrow form tight. Branches that fall out of shape from wind or snow damage should be pruned out or tied back in where possible.
ASPECT: Full sun to partial shade.
FLOWERING: April – May.
HARDINESS: -10 to -15 °C (14 to 5 °F).

6–12 m (20–39 ft)

4–10 m (13–33 ft)

EUCALYPTUS PAUCIFLORA SUBSP. NIPHOPHILA
Snow gum
MYRTACEAE

Many of the species of eucalyptus can grow into huge trees, but this sub-species of snow gum is a small evergreen tree, making it an ideal ornamental tree for a small garden. It has attractive flaking bark in different shades, from silvery-green to grey and cream, giving it year-round interest. Growing it as a multi-stemmed tree adds to its attractiveness. The young foliage is oval-shaped, while the mature foliage becomes narrow, or sickle-shaped and glaucous (blue-grey), and as with all eucalyptus the foliage is scented. Small creamy-white flowers in summer are very attractive to bees.

Pruning should be carried out in late winter, or early spring, removing any branches growing in unwanted directions. Eucalyptus can also be coppiced to produce juvenile foliage, or a multi-stemmed specimen, and can be pruned hard, back to around 30 cm (12 in) from the base.
ASPECT: Full sun to partial shade.
FLOWERING: May – July.
HARDINESS: -10 to -15 °C (14 to 5 °F).

4–5 m (13–16 ft)

3–4 m (10–13 ft)

The green spires of pencil cypress provide a distinctively Mediterranean feel

Cupressus sempervirens

Eucalyptus pauciflora subsp. *niphophila*

Laurus nobilis 'Angustifolia'

JUNIPERUS OXYCEDRUS
Prickly juniper
CUPRESSACEAE

An evergreen shrub or small tree with extremely prickly foliage, this is a plant naturally found growing in the dry Mediterranean lowlands and mountains, making it very drought-tolerant. It forms beautiful small trees with silver-brown, peeling bark.

It is quite ornamental. The leaves are reduced to needle-like structures to lessen water loss. They have two lines on their upper surface, which are actually stomata furrows. These give the leaves a silvery appearance. It has brown-red, berry-like, rounded seed cones. You will need both male and female plants if these cones are to be produced, as the plants are not self-fertile. It needs a sunny aspect as it is a plant that does not do well in shade.

ASPECT: Full sun.
FLOWERING: Flowers are insignificant.
HARDINESS: -5 to -10 °C (23 to 14 °F).

 1–6 m (3–20 ft)

2–3 m (7–10 ft)

LAURUS NOBILIS
Bay tree
LAURACEAE

This is an aromatic evergreen that will make a large tree if left to its own devices.

It has traditionally been clipped and trained as topiary, so can withstand regular pruning, making it ideal for growing in containers in a courtyard or in a gravel garden. It has attractive dark green, glossy leaves, producing pale yellow clusters of flowers in the leaf axils in spring.

It is a must for a herb garden, where it can also be grown in a container or regularly pruned to keep it to a desired, manageable size. The leaves can be used as a seasoning both fresh and dried, giving fragrance to many dishes, particularly soups and stews.

There is also a form with golden-yellow leaves, *Laurus nobilis* 'Aurea', and a linear-leaved form, 'Angustifolia'.

ASPECT: Full sun.
FLOWERING: April – May.
HARDINESS: -5 to -10 °C (23 to 14 °F).

 1–10 m (3–33 ft)

50 cm–8 m (20 in–26 ft)

OLEA EUROPAEA
Olive
OLEACEAE

The olive is a small tree that has been cultivated for thousands of years, but whose exact origins are not known. It is thought to be from the Mediterranean, as fossil pollen records have been found in this area.

From these early species the cultivars that have been produced number in their hundreds.

Visiting some of the old olive groves in places like Crete, Greece, Italy and Spain, with their ancient cultivated trees (some estimated to around 2,000 years old), with wide, gnarly, short trunks and thick branches from hundreds of years of pruning back to improve the yield is quite remarkable. Some of these old groves are being developed and the trees uprooted,

but thankfully many are reused and replanted, and surprisingly for such old and large trees they transplant quite well. Many are just being replaced with newer, better-yielding cultivars.

Olive trees have a smooth silvery-grey trunk when young. This becomes rougher and darker with age. It is an evergreen tree, with leaves that are quite variable, from oblong-lanceolate to elliptical-ovate. They are dark green above and whitish-grey underneath. Clusters of small, creamy-white, four-petalled flowers are borne from the leaf axils in late spring to early summer, and in most years some olives will be produced, but they rarely ripen to their mature black colour.

Olives should not be eaten straight from the tree, as they are bitter-tasting and have a white, milky sap. They need to

be cured with salt and fermented to make them palatable. Green olives are picked and cured at full size, but immature, while black olives are collected when fully ripe.

Olive trees are particularly ornamental and can be grown in large containers in a nice sunny spot in a patio or courtyard garden. They also look great growing in a gravel garden, or as a specimen tree. My own garden wouldn't be without one.

ASPECT: Full sun.

FLOWERING: May – June.

HARDINESS: -5 to -10 °C (23 to 14 °F).

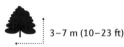
3–7 m (10–23 ft)

2–4 m (7–13 ft)

PINUS HALEPENSIS
Aleppo pine
PINACEAE

There are many pines that would be suitable for the bigger garden, but *Pinus halepensis* is a good all-round conifer. It is a medium-sized tree, evergreen (as are all pines), and has a fairly open, delicate-looking canopy with an upswept habit to the branches. It has bright green, twisted needles in pairs, and produces orange-brown, pointed cones, which reflex back along its branches. Their trunks are grey when young, becoming reddish-brown and fissured when mature.

ASPECT: Full sun.

FLOWERING: During spring, but inconspicuous.

HARDINESS: -10 to -15 °C (14 to 5 °F).

5–10 m (16–33 ft)

4–6 m (13–20 ft)

QUERCUS SUBER
Cork oak
FAGACEAE

If you have the space this is a beautiful medium-sized tree to grow. Most oaks make huge trees, and although the cork

Sculpted over centuries, these ancient olives have a majestic quality

Olea europaea

oak can eventually get quite large, it is fairly slow-growing, and well worth its space.

If I could only have two trees in my garden, one would be an olive and the other would be a cork oak. They are certainly a talking point.

It is an evergreen tree with unmistakable, characteristically deeply fissured corky bark, which extends all along its branches and contrasts well with the mid-green leathery leaves. These are shiny above and glaucous green below, with very variable leaf margins, from a sharply toothed margin to an entire and smooth one. Not a tree grown for its flowers, it does have very attractive acorns, matt green, and held in cups that are covered in very loose felted scales, giving them a shaggy, hairy look.

The cork oak is a tree grown for its harvestable bark (cork), which is regularly removed, like the way sheep are sheared for their wool. Cork is naturally both waterproof and fire-retardant. The bark from cork oaks is harvested roughly every nine years, during May and August, once the trees are more than 20 years old, normally from 25 years old. This is a job carried out by skilled workers (*descortiçadores*), with special wide-bladed axes (*machada*). I have watched this being done. The axe is hit into the tree, and the cutters know by the sound the axe makes that they are going in at the correct depth, so as not to damage the tree's cambium layer.

This harvest continues throughout the life of the tree, around 200 years, so up to 12–15 harvests are possible. The quality of the cork improves with the age of the tree. The cork is boiled to clean and soften it, before the bottle corks are pressed out. The remaining cork is crushed and used in other cork products. Portugal and Spain produce more than half of the world's cork (along with north Africa) from more than 2 million hectares (4.9 million acres) of cork oak forest.

Tamarix ramosissima

ASPECT: Full sun.
FLOWERING: Spring, but fairly inconspicuous.
HARDINESS: -5 to -10 °C (23 to 14 °F).

 5–10 m (16–33 ft)

3–8 m (10–26 ft)

TAMARIX RAMOSISSIMA
Tamarisk

TAMARICACEAE

Tamarisk is a deciduous large shrub or small tree with a very different appearance from most other shrubs or small trees. It is a plant that has fine, feathery foliage on long arching stems, which will soften a planting scheme around it.

Tamarisk species flower either in spring, summer or autumn. *Tamarix ramosissima* is a summer and autumn flowering species, when it will produce its small, pink terminal racemes, which transform the whole plant, covering it almost completely in these beautifully delicate pink flowers, at a time when there are not many other plants flowering.

Because they are mostly shrubby, they need to be pruned to form a single stem. Any pruning of this particular species should be done in late winter.

Tamarisks are great drought-tolerant plants and are also particularly good for growing in coastal areas, as they accept salty sea air and windy conditions. The one thing they do not like is chalky soils.

ASPECT: Full sun.
FLOWERING: July – September.
HARDINESS: -5 to -10 °C (23 to 14°F).

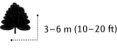 3–6 m (10–20 ft)

3–4 m (10–13 ft)

OVERLEAF Old olive grove

Glossary

Alternate Arranged at each node on different sides of a stem. Not opposite

Annual Completes its life cycle in one year

Anther The pollen-bearing male reproductive organ

Axil The junction of leaf and stem

Axillary Arising in the axil

Basal Located at the base of the plant or stem. Usually leaves

Biennial Germinates and grows in its first year. Flowers and completes its life cycle in the second year

Bract A modified leaf usually at the base of a flower. Sometimes more showy than the actual flower

Bulb An underground storage organ made up of swollen leaf bases

Calyx The outer parts of a flower, the sepals

Cambium The layer of cells below the bark of roots and stem that divide to produce new tissue

Climber Also known as lianes, these are plants with long trailing stems modified to climb by hooks/thorns, suckers and tendrils

Corm Resembling a bulb, but replaced annually on top of the old one

Cultivar A new plant produced in cultivation rather than in the wild and which has to be propagated vegetatively to remain true

Cuticle Waxy surface of a leaf limiting water loss

Cyathium A typical inflorescence in the genus *Euphorbia*

Deciduous A plant that sheds its leaves at the end of each growing season, renewing them at the start of the next season

Dioecious Having male and female flowers on separate plants

Endemic Restricted to a specific geographic region

Evergreen A plant that retains most of its leaves throughout the year

Evapotranspiration The process by which water is transferred from the land to the air by evaporation and from plants by transpiration

Floriferous Plants producing many flowers

Genus A group of species with similar characters, e.g. *Cistus*

Glaucous Bluish-grey in colour

Globular Spherical or rounded in shape

Habitat Place where a plant grows, which is often characteristic of a species

Herbaceous A plant that is not woody and dies back to around ground level in winter

Hybrid A plant resulting from the cross-fertilisation of two different individual species

Inflorescence The flowering part of a plant

Lanceolate Having a narrow outline, usually widest in the middle, tapering towards the tip. Lance-shaped

Lateral At the side

Lax Loose and spreading

Linear Long, thin leaves. Grass-like

Maquis Similar to garigue vegetation, but denser and with larger plants

Margin Outer edge, usually of a leaf

Monocarpic Flowering once and then dying

Monoecious Male and female flowers on the same plant, but separate

Native A plant growing in a place where it was not introduced by humans or animals

Node The place on a stem where the leaves are attached

Obovate Oval, but widest above the middle

Panicle A branching stem of stalked flowers

Perennial Any plant living for 3 years or more. Usually flowering annually, but not always in the first year

Petiole The stalk between the leaf and stem

Photosynthesis The process by which plants use sunlight to convert carbon dioxide into the sugars they use as food

Pinnate With leaflets arranged either side of a single stalk

Prostrate Growing flat on the ground

Racemes Flowers on separate stalks making up clusters along a central stem

Rhizome A creeping stem, which can be above or below ground

Rosette A cluster of leaves radiating from the same point, usually basal

Sclerophyllous A plant with leathery evergreen leaves designed to reduce water loss. A common adaptation in the Mediterranean region

Semi-evergreen Plants that lose their leaves for a short period of time between the old foliage falling and new foliage growth

Sepal A segment of the calyx

Sessile Stalkless

Shrub A perennial with woody, much-branched stems

Species Plants with the members having similar characteristic to each other

Spine A rigid sharp structure on a stem or leaf

Stamen The male part of a flower, consisting of both filament and anther

Steppe Landscape mainly made up of grasses and low herbaceous plants

Stigma The top of the style which receives the pollen

Sub-shrub A small plant with a woody base and herbaceous top

Succulent Plants with fleshy parts that store water, e.g. cactus

Tendril A thread-like modified leaflet, used to help a plants support and climbing

Tepal Used when petals and sepals look alike. Usually in the flowers of bulbous plants, e.g. tulips

Tree A perennial, usually with a single woody stem

Tuber A swollen underground stem or root

Umbel An inflorescence with several flowers all arising from the same point

Undulate With a wavy margin or surface

Variety Plants that often occur naturally and usually come true from seed. See Cultivar

Whorl The arrangement of flowers or leaves that circle around the same point on a stem

Woody perennial See Shrub

Xerophyte, xeromorphic An adaption to survival in dry and arid desert-like conditions

Vegetatively Propagating a plant from parts other than its reproductive part, i.e. roots

Further reading

Chatto, Beth.
The Dry Garden.
ORION, 1998

The Beth Chatto Handbook: Beth Chatto's Descriptive List of Unusual Plants.
THE BETH CHATTO GARDENS LTD, 2015.

Filippi, Olivier.
The Dry Gardening Handbook: Plants and Practices for a Changing Climate.
THAMES & HUDSON, 2013

Gildemeister, Heidi.
Mediterranean Gardening: A Waterwise Approach.
UNIVERSITY OF CALIFORNIA PRESS, 1995

Gardening the Mediterranean Way:
Practical Solutions for Summer-dry Climates.
THAMES & HUDSON, 2004

Hall, Tony.
Wild Plants of Southern Spain: A Guide to The Native Plants of Andalucía.
THE ROYAL BOTANIC GARDENS, KEW, 2017

Latymer, Hugo.
The Mediterranean Gardener.
FRANCES LINCOLN LTD IN ASSOCIATION WITH THE ROYAL BOTANIC GARDENS, KEW, 1990

Payne, Graham.
Garden Plants for Mediterranean Climates.
THE CROWOOD PRESS, 2002

Royal Horticultural Society.
Gardeners' Encyclopedia of Plants and Flowers.
DORLING KINDERSLEY, 1990

Rix, Martyn.
Subtropical and Dry Climate Plants: The Definitive Practical Guide.
MITCHELL BEAZLEY IN ASSOCIATION WITH THE ROYAL BOTANIC GARDENS, KEW, 2006.

Websites

Plants For A Future: pfaf.org

Royal Horticultural Society: rhs.org.uk

World Checklist of Selected Plant Families: wcsp.science.kew.org

Flowering by month

JANUARY

Clematis cirrhosa

Viburnum tinus

FEBRUARY

Acacia dealbata

Clematis cirrhosa

Daphne laureola

Viburnum tinus

MARCH

Acacia dealbata

Celtis australis

Clematis cirrhosa

Daphne laureola

Euphorbia spp. & cvs

Viburnum tinus

APRIL

Acacia dealbata	Halimium atriplicifolium
Acer monspessulanum	Iberis gibraltarica
Ajuga reptans	Laurus nobilis
Akebia quinata	Lonicera etrusca 'Superba'
Bergenia spp. & cvs	Phillyrea angustifolia
Celtis australis	Pinus halepensis
Cercis siliquastrum	Pistacia lentiscus
Chamaerops humilis	Quercus suber
Cistus spp.	Rhamnus alaternus 'Argenteovarigata'
Coronilla valentina	Rosmarinus officinalis
Digitalis obscura	Thymus spp. & cvs
Echium spp.	Viburnum tinus
Euphorbia spp. & cvs	

Clematis cirrhosa

MAY

Acanthus mollis	Echium spp.	Nepeta × faasenii
Acer monspessulanum	Erigeron karvinskianus	Olea europaea
Achillea millefolium	Eschscholzia californica	Phillyrea angustifolia
Ajuga reptans	Eucalyptus pauciflora subsp. niphophila	Phlomis spp. & cvs
Akebia quinata	Euphorbia spp. & cvs	Phoenix canariensis
Bergenia spp. & cvs	Genista lydia	Pinus halepensis
Cerastium tomentosum	Geranium spp. & cvs	Pistacia lentiscus
Cercis siliquastrum	Halimium atriplicifolium	Quercus suber
Chamaerops humilis	Helianthemum apenninum	Rhamnus alaternus 'Argenteovarigata'
Cistus spp.	Iberis gibraltarica	Rosmarinus officinalis
Convolvulus cneorum	Jasminum humile	Salvia spp. & cvs
Coronilla valentina	Laurus nobilis	Thymus spp. & cvs
Crambe maritima	Lonicera etrusca 'Superba'	Ugni molinae
Dianella tasmanica	Medicago arborea	Wisteria sinensis
Digitalis obscura	Melaleuca pallidus	

Cistus 'Grayswood Pink'

Lavandula stoechas 'Kew Red'

JUNE

Acanthus mollis	Cistus spp.	Geranium spp. & cvs	Origanum dictamnus
Acca sellowiana	Convolvulus cneorum	Halimium atriplicifolium	Papaver rupifragum
Achillea millefolium	Cordyline australis	Helianthemum apenninum	Phlomis spp. & cvs
Aeonium arboreum	Crambe maritima	Hypericum balearicum	Phoenix canariensis
Ajuga reptans	Dianella tasmanica	Iberis gibraltarica	Rosmarinus officinalis
Albizia julibrissin	Digitalis obscura	Jasminum humile	Salvia spp. & cvs
Akebia quinata	Echium sp.	Lavandula spp. & cvs	Santolina chamaecyparissus
Allium spp.	Erigeron karvinskianus	Libertia peregrinans	Senecio cineraria
Aloe striatula	Eryngium spp. & cvs	Lonicera etrusca 'Superba'	Sideritis syriaca
Asphodeline lutea	Eschscholzia californica	Marrubium 'All Hallows Green'	Sisyrinchium striatum
Asphodelus alba	Eucalyptus pauciflora subsp. niphophila	Medicago arborea	Teucrium fruticans
Brachyglottis 'Sunshine'	Euphorbia spp. & cvs	Melaleuca pallidus	Thymus spp. & cvs
Buddleja alternifolia	Euryops tysonii	Myrtus communis	Trachelospermum jasminoides
Bupleurum fruticosum	Ferula communis	Nassella tenuissima	Tulbaghia violacea
Carpenteria californica	Festuca glauca	Nepeta × faasenii	Ugni molinae
Centranthus ruber	Ficus carica	Olea europaea	Verbena bonariensis
Cerastium tomentosum	Genista lydia	Olearia macrodonta	Wisteria sinensis
Chamaerops humilis			

Bergenia cordifolia **'Purpurea'**

Foeniculum vulgare

JULY

Acanthus mollis	Cerastium tomentosum	Helianthemum apenninum	Phlomis spp. & cvs
Acca sellowiana	Cistus spp.	Helichrysum italicum	Punica granatum
Achillea millefolium	Convolvulus cneorum	Hesperaloe parviflora	Romneya coulteri
Aeonium arboreum	Cordyline australis	Hypericum balearicum	Rosa sempervirens
Agapanthus spp. & cvs	Crambe maritima	Iberis gibraltarica	Rosmarinus officinalis
Albizia julibrissin	Digitalis obscura	Lavandula spp. & cvs	Salvia spp. & cvs
Allium spp.	Echinops ritro	Libertia peregrinans	Santolina chamaecyparissus
Aloe striatula	Echium spp.	Lonicera etrusca 'Superba'	Sedum sediforme
Artemisia absinthium	Erigeron karvinskianus	Marrubium 'All Hallows Green'	Senecio cineraria
Asphodeline lutea	Eryngium spp. & cvs	Melaleuca pallidus	Sideritis syriaca
Asphodelus alba	Eschscholzia californica	Myrtus communis	Sisyrinchium striatum
Ballota pseudodictamnus	Eucalyptus pauciflora subsp. niphophila	Nandina domestica	Stachys byzantina
Brachyglottis 'Sunshine'	Euphorbia spp. & cvs	Nassella tenuissima	Tamarix ramosissima
Buddleja alternifolia	Euryops tysonii	Nepeta × faasenii	Teucrium fruticans
Buddleja davidii	Ferula communis	Nerium oleander	Thymus spp. & cvs
Bupleurum fruticosum	Festuca glauca	Olearia macrodonta	Trachelospermum jasminoides
Butia capitata	Ficus carica	Ophiopogon planiscapus 'Nigrescens'	Tulbaghia violacea
Calamintha nepeta	Foeniculum vulgare	Origanum dictamnus	Ugni molinae
Campsis radicans	Genista aetnensis	Papaver rupifragum	Verbena bonariensis
Carpenteria californica	Geranium spp. & cvs	Pennisetum alopecuroides	Vinca difformis
Centranthus ruber	Halimium atriplicifolium	Perovskia 'Blue Spire'	Wisteria sinensis
			Zauschneria californica

AUGUST

Acanthus mollis	Asphodelus alba	Ceratostigma willmottianum	Geranium spp. & cvs
Acca sellowiana	Ballota pseudodictamnus	Cordyline australis	Halimium atriplicifolium
Achillea millefolium	Buddleja davidii	Echinops ritro	Helichrysum italicum
Aeonium arboreum	Bupleurum fruticosum	Erigeron karvinskianus	Hesperaloe parviflora
Agapanthus spp. & cvs	Butia capitata	Eryngium spp. & cvs	Hypericum balearicum
Albizia julibrissin	Calamintha nepeta	Euryops tysonii	Lavandula spp. & cvs
Allium spp.	Campsis radicans	Fiscus carica	Myrtus communis
Aloe striatula	Centranthus ruber	Foeniculum vulgare	Nandina domestica
Artemisia absinthium	Cerastium tomentosum	Genista aetensis	Nassella tenuissima
			Nepeta × faasenii

Fragrant plants

FLOWERS

Bulbs	Shrubs
Asphodeline lutea	Argyrocytisus battandieri
Narcissus papyraceus	Carpenteria californica
Tulbaghia violacea	Coronilla valentina subsp. glauca
Climbers	Daphne laureola
Akebia quinata	Eriobotrya japonica
Clematis cirrhosa	Euryops tysonii
Lonicera etrusca 'Superba'	Genista aetnensis
Solanum crispum 'Glasnevin'	Jasminum humile
Trachelospermum jasminoides	Lavandula spp.
Wisteria sinensis	Melianthus major
	Myrtus communis
Perennials	Nerium oleander
Crambe maritima	Phillyrea angustifolia
Romneya coulteri	
	Trees
	Acacia dealbata

FOLIAGE

Bulbs	Shrubs
Allium spp.	Cistus spp.
	Ficus carica
Perennials	Helichrysum italicum
Artemisia absinthium	Lavandula spp.
Calamintha nepeta	Melianthus comosus
Foeniculum vulgare	Melianthus major
Geranium spp.	Myrtus communis
Nepeta × faasenii	Origanum dictamnus
Salvia spp.	Perovskia 'Blue Spire'
	Phlomis spp.
Trees	Pistacia lentiscus
Eucalyptus pauciflora subsp. niphophila	Rosmarinus officinalis
Juniperus oxycedrus	Santolina chamaecyparissus
Laurus nobilis	Thymus spp.

Narcissus papyraceus

OPPOSITE *Daphne laureola*

Trachelospermum jasminoides

Eucalyptus leaves

Plants for wildlife

Bulbs	Perennials	Shrubs
Agapanthus	Achillea millefolium	Buddleja alternifolia
Allium spp.	Calamintha nepeta	Buddleja davidii
	Echinops ritro	Buddleja globosa
Climbers	Echium spp.	Bupleurum fruticosum
Campsis radicans	Erigeron karvinskianus	Cistus spp.
Clematis cirrhosa	Eryngium spp.	Lavandula spp.
Lonicera etrusca 'Superba'	Ferula communis	Myrtus communis
	Geranium spp.	Olearia macrodonta
Trees	Kniphofia spp.	Origanum dictamnus
Eucalyptus pauciflora subsp. niphophila	Nepeta × faasenii	Rosmarinus officinalis
	Papaver rupifragum	Sedum spp.
	Salvia spp.	Teucrium chamaedrys
	Verbena bonariensis	Thymus spp.

Honey bee (*Apis mellifera*)

Bumblebee (*Bombus terrestris*) on *Echinops* flower

Comma butterfly (*Polygonia c-album*)

OPPOSITE Painted lady butterfly (*Vanessa cardui*)

OVERLEAF Eryngiums and geraniums

Hoverfly (*Volucella zonaria*)

Index

Entries with a photograph are indicated by a **bold** page number.